D0930607

From Orphans to Champions:
THE STORY OF
DEMATHA'S MORGAN WOOTTEN

From Orphans to Champions

THE STORY OF DEMATHA'S MORGAN WOOTTEN

Morgan Wootten
and Bill Gilbert

NEW YORK

Atheneum

1980

Library of Congress Cataloging in Publication Data
Wootten, Morgan.
   From orphans to champions.
      1. Wootten, Morgan.   2. Basketball coaches—United
States—Biography.   3. DeMatha Catholic High School.
I. Gilbert, Bill, 1931–   joint author.   II. Title.
GV884.W67A33   1979   796.32'3'0924 [B]   79-63847
ISBN 0-689-11011-1

Published simultaneously in Canada by McClelland and Stewart Ltd.
Composition by American–Stratford Graphic Services, Inc.,
Brattleboro, Vermont
Printed and bound by Fairfield Graphics,
Fairfield, Pennsylvania
Designed by Kathleen Carey
First Printing October 1979
Second Printing February 1980

This book is dedicated to my number-one team of all time—my wife, Kathy, and our children, Cathy, Carol, Tricia, Brendan and Joey.

And to God, for allowing me to become a teacher and a coach.

Acknowledgments

I could not begin this book without acknowledging the deep debt I owe so many people for so many reasons:

All the fine young men I have had the privilege of teaching and coaching.

The great coaches who have coached with me and against me.

That special group of coaches who gave so much of their time and wisdom to teach me the game of life as well as basketball, men like John Wooden, Red Auerbach, Joe Gallagher, Jim Kehoe, Vic Bubas, Dean Smith, Norman Sloan, Ken Loeffler, Bud Millikan, John Ryall and so many others.

My mother, for passing to me her intense drive and love of competition, and my father, for teaching me to tell the truth and to be myself—always.

My sisters, Clare and Lee Lee, and my brother, Angus, who all helped in so many ways.

Acknowledgments

My Uncle Jack and Uncle Robert, who were like second fathers to me.

To four physicians and friends, Doctors Gaffney, Sullivan, Scalessa and Lavine.

To the parents of all the young men I have had the privilege of teaching and coaching.

To John Moylan, one of the nation's most respected high school principals, and his outstanding staff.

To all the great men and women who were my teachers from the first grade on.

The three men who coached me in high school and college, Reno Continetti, Tony Creme and Frank Rubini.

The Holy Cross nuns who gave me my start as a coach.

The Christian Brothers, who gave me my start as a teacher and enabled me to advance my career as a coach.

The Trinitarians and all the DeMatha family, for their help and support through the years.

And to so many other people, too numerous to mention, who touched my life and inspired me to touch others' lives.

Contents

---

ix

Foreword

BY RED AUERBACH

I don't mind writing a foreword for a book by someone like Morgan Wootten. He's the kind of person you're glad to write about because you believe in him and in what he does. Every high school boy or girl should be lucky enough to have him as a coach.

I first met Morgan more than twenty years ago, when he was just starting out at DeMatha Catholic High School, and he is still doing the things he did then: emphasizing the fundamentals, preaching teamwork, quoting poetry and philosophy and at the same time listening to his players and learning from what they can teach him. He's also a good poker player, but he smokes lousy cigars.

Morgan is my kind of guy, a man I'd want coaching my own kids because of what he considers important and the kind of example he sets. I'm not underestimating his record as a winner. As one whose teams have won more than a thousand games, I want to win as much as the next guy, probably more. What makes Morgan one of America's top coaches in any sport, however, is that he strikes that beautiful balance; he doesn't emphasize winning at the exclusion of everything else—or vice versa. Things should be that balanced at every level of athletic competition, but especially at the high school level and below.

That's what makes Morgan a winner in the record book and in the eyes of everyone familiar with his accomplishments over the years. He knows that success takes more than just the ability to bounce a basketball and put it through a hoop. His teams have always been able to do those things better than their opponents, and his players have been able to go on from that basketball success to success of every kind in their adult lives.

For all these reasons, this book is a gold mine of information for a lot of people—parents, young athletes and coaches. Morgan tells you the importance of being what he calls "a good person." He tells you the stories behind his greatest accomplishments, and they are too numerous to mention here. He tells coaches how to build and maintain a special program, preparations which can be applied to any sport. He tells parents and athletes what it takes to achieve success in athletics—or in other fields—and he tells athletes how to maximize their chances of winning a scholarship to college.

It's just like having one of the most successful coaches in history sit down with you in your home and tell you everything you need to know to be successful, while throwing in some delightful, very human yarns of his own experiences along the way—and he's had some hilarious and some very touching ones.

This book is a winner because Morgan is a winner in every important way. I'm glad to be part of his book, just as I'm glad to be a part of his life.

RED AUERBACH
President and General Manager—Boston Celtics

Introduction

MEET MORGAN WOOTTEN

Morgan Wootten may be the most successful coach in basketball history. His teams have won 626 games and lost only 88. His won-lost mark of 88 percent is believed to be the highest in basketball history, even better than that of two legends—Red Auerbach of the Boston Celtics and John Wooden of UCLA. Ninety of his players have gone on to successful careers as college athletes and twenty players and assistant coaches have become college coaches. His teams have won four national and five national Catholic championships, plus more than fifty other championships, and one team has gone undefeated. He has been the subject of lavish spreads in *Sports Illustrated* ("The Wizard of Washington"), *Time* and *People* magazines. He has been featured several times on national television, invited to the White House and enshrined with his team in the Basketball Hall of Fame. He has done more than put DeMatha High School, near Washington,

D.C., on the basketball map. He has made it the capital.

That record of success, almost unmatched in any sport at any level, is not why this book has been written, however. There are winning coaches in every sport, although their records may not approach Wootten's. Morgan Wootten stands out for other reasons.

He has produced championship players and championship teams, yet he tells his players basketball should be no higher than the fourth most important thing in their lives.

He gave the world Olympic stars such as Adrian Dantley and Kenny Carr, who combined to lead the United States team to the gold medal for basketball in the 1976 Olympics, yet he is prouder of what his players have done in their academic achievements and their professional careers, and proudest of all of the fact that every single DeMatha player in the past nineteen years, starter or substitute, has won a full four-year college scholarship in his senior year.

He is the most famous high school coach in the world in any sport, yet he'd rather be considered a teacher than a coach. He spends more time in the classroom as a teacher of world history—three hours every morning—than on the basketball court.

He is a 100 percent disciplinarian, yet many of his players call him by his first name, play tennis and cards with him and openly imitate him at team parties, while the coach laughs louder than anyone else.

He has inspired his teams and his players to heights they never dreamed possible, yet he tells them the most important achievement in life is to be a good person. He believes in building men, not just players, in preparing someone for life, not just basketball.

That's Morgan Wootten.

I first met Morgan when we were classmates in the ninth grade at Gonzaga High School in Washington, D.C. We were also teammates, but not in basketball, football or baseball—in debating. We won the championship, even went undefeated, but though Wootten had to wait thirty-two years for his next undefeated season, it took him far less time than that to make his mark.

In less than a decade after that ninth-grade championship, with a philosophy based on the works and words of Red Auerbach, John Wooden, Knute Rockne, Vince Lombardi, Harry Truman, Winston Churchill, St. Francis of Assisi, Rudyard Kipling, Douglas MacArthur and the heroes of ancient Greece and Rome, he was well on his way to becoming the best high school coach anywhere in anything. His teams at DeMatha have made that school the UCLA, the Yankees, the Pittsburgh Steelers of high school basketball, capable in 1977/78 of winning the national championship with a record of twenty-seven wins and no losses.

How Morgan Wootten has achieved that success story, however, is as impressive as the record itself. He has done it while constantly reminding his athletes that basketball should never be the most important thing in their lives. When you play for Morgan Wootten, he tells you that your priorities should be:

1. God
2. Family
3. School
4. Basketball

"If you came to DeMatha because basketball is the most important thing in your life," he tells his players at the start of each season, "then you're not going to make it here, because your priorities are out of order."

God. The wall decorations and books on the shelves of the Wootten home testify to the emphasis on religion in the Wootten family. "Show me a young athlete with a spiritual commitment," Wootten quotes another successful coach, Bud Wilkinson, "and I'll show you a winner."

Family. At day's end, you walk behind him through the door of his home near DeMatha in the Maryland suburbs outside Washington and see five kids competing with each other to be the first to greet him with an enthusiastic hug and kiss, while his wife, Kathy, waits her turn.

School. A conversation with him in his cluttered and cramped office just off the playing floor at DeMatha (coaches' offices are always described as "cluttered and cramped" because they always are) is interrupted repeatedly with phone calls and unscheduled visits from former players, coaches and history students—young men making it in their chosen fields, thanks in part to the Wootten emphasis on schoolwork to prepare for the real world.

Basketball. In that typical coach's office, the mementos, the bulletin board crowded with clippings, the small round table where coaches and scouts from twenty-five or thirty colleges a week visit to look at the latest Wootten bumper crop of future college stars, where Notre Dame's Digger Phelps sat just two hours before you—all these tell the story of athletic accomplishment.

It's a special record of achievement, attained by a special approach to others and to life itself. When you witness it—in its day-in, day-out unfolding—you realize that it was no wonder your high school debating team went un-defeated. With Morgan Wootten, such things were meant to be.

BILL GILBERT
Washington, D.C.
March, 1979

From Orphans to Champions:
THE STORY OF
DEMATHA'S MORGAN WOOTTEN

Orphans and Champions

He ain't heavy, Father—he's my brother.
—SLOGAN FOR BOYS' TOWN

Morgan Wootten never had any intention of becoming a coach. He was double-teamed by a friend and the Good Lord without even realizing it, but now, nearly thirty years later, he remembers how it happened.

It was mid-March of 1951. Morgan Wootten was nineteen and, with his friend Tommy Clark, was busy with the concerns of many nineteen-year-olds of the day: college, athletics and, in general, enjoying life while keeping his fingers crossed that his navy reserves unit, which was also Tommy's, would not be called to active duty in the new Korean War.

Morgan and Tommy had been buddies since their grade school days together at Saint Michael's Parish in Silver Spring, Maryland, just outside Washington, D.C. Tommy had gone on to athletic stardom as an All-Metropolitan football player at Saint John's High and had also done well in basketball and baseball. Morgan, after transferring from Gonzaga High School, had gradu-

3

ated from Montgomery Blair High with a decidedly average basketball and football record—he had seldom gotten to start a game. Now he was attending Montgomery
Junior College near his home, preparing for a career as a
lawyer, convinced he could out-argue anybody due to
that ninth-grade debating championship. He also finally
had found a sport in which he could start—boxing.

It was then that Morgan's uncle, Jack Erly, who
worked with the Police Boys' Club in Washington, called
to ask if Morgan knew anyone who could help some orphans play baseball—Saint Joseph's Home for Boys
needed a coach. Morgan had the perfect choice: Tommy
Clark.

Tommy seemed less than enthusiastic, but the two of
them drove over to the orphanage on Bunker Hill Road
near the Maryland-Washington line in Morgan's beat-up
1941 Buick that had already seen more than a hundred
thousand miles. On the way, Morgan turned from the
wheel and said, "You know, Tommy, you'll be a nat-
ural for this."

Tommy hedged. "Maybe you could do it."

"No, I'm not a baseball man, but you are. You played
it and I don't know a thing about it."

"Well," Tommy said, "we'll talk to the Sister."

"I should have known right then that something was
up," Morgan says today.

The old Buick with its crew-cut occupants headed up
the long, winding driveway to a big red brick building
which sat alone at the top of a hill surrounded by large
fields, a rundown swimming pool close by. Morgan
thought, "So this is what an orphanage looks like." He
expected Father Flanagan, played by Spencer Tracy, to
come around the corner any minute.

The pair headed inside, noticing the clean but plain
rooms and hallways, and eventually arrived at the office
of Sister Batilde of the Order of the Holy Cross, Mother

4

Superior of the orphanage. She was an older nun, dressed in full black habit and big white headpiece. On one wall hung a picture of Pope Pius XII, the only picture in her office.

The meeting between the three of them began routinely enough, with Morgan pushing Tommy for the job, but then the conversation took an unexpected turn. Tommy nodded toward his friend and said, "Hey, Sister, he's a candidate, too."

Sister Batilde wasn't particular. "All I know," she said, "is I need a baseball coach."

Tommy became more emphatic—"Sister, he's your man"—and began a heavy sales pitch about the many virtues of young Mister Wootten.

Morgan says today he knows his pal didn't really believe all that he was saying. "By then he wasn't fooling me. He was just trying to save his own skin and get out of there." It worked, though. Clark, a successful salesman today, poured it on, and finally the Sister said, "He certainly sounds like the man for the job," turned to Morgan and told him the terms. Seventy-five dollars a month. Practice every day, including weekends. Helps to keep the boys occupied, you know. And, oh, yes, you'll have to supervise evening study hall for the seventh and eighth graders every night.

Then she smiled at Morgan and said, "See you Monday."

That's how he became a coach. But somehow . . .

I don't remember ever accepting the job. I really don't. I got sandbagged so fast and so hard I never knew what hit me. All of a sudden I was a coach. Absolutely unqualified, no coaching experience of any kind, handling the one sport I knew nothing about, and working with kids not much younger than myself. It was definitely not the formula for success. But I'm convinced today it was God working His will.

On our first day of practice, I saw what it was like to coach a team at an orphanage. We had a couple of bats, taped together because they were cracked, and two balls, both waterlogged. They seemed to weigh ten pounds each and were as hard as cement. Throwing them was more like shotputting than baseball. That was our equipment—all of it.

I thought the seventy-five dollars a month would help pay for all that gas and oil driving back and forth from Silver Spring to Mount Rainier and cover a hamburger or two for dinner, but part of that handsome salary went to buy equipment, what I couldn't beg or borrow from friends.

Help? Not at an orphanage. There isn't any. You're on your own, and it's not the happy-go-lucky life that Bing Crosby made it appear in *Going My Way*. There aren't any parents to help you coach because there aren't any parents, period. The budget won't afford any paid assistants because there isn't any money. For that reason, there isn't any budget, either.

So you're out there all alone trying to teach, trying to maintain discipline, trying to keep the infielders and outfielders occupied while you pitch batting practice and trying—above all— to keep the fun in it for everybody.

It would be nice to say that the opening of my coaching career overcame these staggering odds and we won the championship of the Catholic Youth Organization we were in. The truth is I didn't overcome anything. We never even won a game. We finished with no wins and sixteen losses. To make it worse, we never even came close. We lost games by twenty or thirty runs, games that were being called in the third inning because of the league's time limit of two and a half hours. Can you imagine that? Two and a half hours and still only the third inning.

The funny thing is, I thought before the season started that we'd be pretty good. That shows you how unqualified I was for the job. I should have picked up a clue from Father Tom Lyons, one of the young priests in Washington. He used to come over and take a few licks against our pitchers after they had progressed to the point where they could pitch batting practice. He used to kill our guys. I was impressed. I thought he was a great hitter. It turned out the reason was our pitching, not his skill with a bat.

I saw him not long ago. He's Bishop Lyons now, a ranking member of the Archdiocese and in charge of its education program. "Bishop," I told him, "I thought you were a great hitter in those days, but I found out I had you badly overrated." With a bishop, you have to be honest.

Nobody had to tell you we were a team of orphans. We looked it. All the other teams had first-class uniforms. We had plain white T-shirts and blue jeans. There was no question about who we were. And we just couldn't get anybody out. The highlight of our season was when we pulled the hidden ball trick and picked a man off second base to end an inning. It was doubly exciting because the other team had the bases loaded at the time. They usually did.

It was a tribute to those boys, though, that they never let up, never stopped coming to practice, always on time, never lost their enthusiasm while getting murdered every

7

time out. They kept having fun and I just told them to keep trying their best—that's all any coach should ask. I told them the same things I tell teams today in rough times: "Show me a lot of class. No moaning, no groaning. No arguing with teammates or anyone else. No complaints about the weather or the umpire or injuries. If we're not good enough now, we'll have to work harder to get better."

I thought sooner or later they'd start laughing in my face because they'd heard it from me a million times and kept doing their best—and there was still no improvement. Everybody's attitude held up, however, and when the season was over, the boys asked me to come back in the fall and coach them in football. How could I refuse? I was learning more from them about other things than they were learning from me about baseball.

Sister Batilde was patient through that whole horrible baseball season, but she never changed her attitude, either. She knew only one thing about sports: You win or lose. She preferred winning, and she showed it immediately—after our first game.

We got ourselves clobbered, 32–0, by Saint Anthony's. We staggered back to the orphanage, still cross-eyed and licking our wounds, when we found, much to our encouragement, that Sister Malathon, in charge of the kitchen, had cold soft drinks waiting for us in the cafeteria.

We stumbled that far and were sitting there thinking we might survive this cruel ordeal after all when Sister Batilde walked in. She lit up a bright smile as she spotted us enjoying our cold drinks and said happily, "You won, Coach?"

"No, Sister," I said. "We lost." I didn't have the guts

to tell her the score, but that was all the information she needed. She ordered the boys to get right up and march themselves straight out to that kitchen and put those drinks back in the refrigerator where they belonged. There were no questions asked. We lost, and that's all she needed to know. We could have lost to the New York Yankees and she would have given us the same treatment. It was a long, dry season.

In the fall, her treatment was better, because we were. I came back. I couldn't stay away. By the time that disastrous baseball season had ended, the boys and I had formed a real affection for each other. Nobody was going to come between us. Losers? No, sir. Not on your life. Zero and sixteen? So what? We were going to lick the world together, and have a great time doing it—and nothing as trivial as a 0–16 record was going to stop us. Besides, football was another story. When they asked me after the season to return in the fall, the boys said, "Come back and coach us in football, Morgan. We're a lot better in that."

They were, too. We went undefeated and won Washington's CYO championship. We got to play a preliminary game before the big annual rivalry between Gonzaga and Saint John's at Griffith Stadium, right there where the Redskins played all their home games. We even won it while carrying a fourth grader in that league of eighth and ninth graders. He was my secret psychological weapon, a half-pint named Scotty Jackson. Any time we weren't moving the ball, I'd put Scotty in and he'd get murdered. I'd look shocked and sad and say to the team, "Would you look at what they just did to poor little Scotty?" Our guys would get so fired up they'd explode

9

and blow the game wide open. Worked every time.

With all those great experiences in football, I became hooked on coaching as a career. I also became hooked on kids. After almost thirty years as a coach and as a history teacher, I still believe in the school of thought which says that all kids are basically good. Some may stray, some may wind up leading terrible lives later, but when we have them, they are still basically good—even the ones in trouble—and some time and understanding is often all they need. I think they have a right to ask that of us.

At Saint Joseph's, most of the kids were orphans and a few were from broken homes. They knew only one male figure in their lives—me. I was with them in football, basketball and baseball and in the study hall at night to help them with their schoolwork. I was barely twenty years old myself, so I was hardly equipped with all of life's answers, but to these guys I was coach, teacher, father, big brother and friend. They were my friends, too. It was a great relationship for all of us, and I learned and benefited and grew as much from it as they did, maybe more.

It was never a problem to motivate those kids. They went to a variety of grade schools in the Archdiocese, a few to this school, a few to that, wherever there was room for some orphans from Saint Joseph's Home. They knew from their classmates what other kids had: a home, new clothes, maybe a room of their own, a real mom and dad and brothers and sisters. And they could compare that to what they came "home" to each afternoon: no mother, no father, life in a dormitory, dinner in a cafeteria instead of around a family table, study hall after supper instead of playing with your brother or going outside to play touch football or talking to your dad or hugging your mom.

These kids didn't have any of that and they knew what they were missing. When they went out to play a championship football game on Thanksgiving Day, they knew what they'd be going home to and what the members of the other team would be doing after the game—in real homes. The Saint Joseph's teams were always up, trying to show the world they were just as good as anyone else, even though they didn't have as much.

I wasn't above emphasizing that they were orphans when I thought it might help our cause. We had no money for our sports programs except what I could scare up on my own, so I started the practice of sending the kids door-to-door in the neighborhood around the orphanage, collecting newspapers and selling them to trash dealers. I drove the boys around in my uncle's pickup truck and kept reminding them, "Now remember, when they answer that door, make sure you tell them you're from Saint Joseph's *Orphanage* and we're trying to scrape up enough money to help you kids play ball."

We scraped up enough money and sympathy to buy the same things all the other teams had: nice uniforms; good, safe equipment and even a pickup truck of our own, brand new, so we could use it as often as we needed to go out collecting papers.

Then there were great folks like Johnny Ryall, a businessman who was always willing to chip in his own money to help kids. After our baseball season brought us together and then that football championship proved we could win, all of us wanted to have a basketball team for the orphanage. However, a gymnasium was like asking for the moon. No chance. We had a small paved area outside —blacktop but no baskets. I went to Johnny Ryall, though, and he whipped out his checkbook in nothing flat to pay for baskets, backboards and poles.

Now the kids had a place to practice—outside—and we could have a basketball team after all. The upshot was not only did we form a team, we went all the way to the CYO quarter-finals. Not bad for a bunch of orphans in their first year of basketball. And we did it against teams which had gyms to practice in. We practiced every day—just as they did—only we practiced outdoors on that pavement. Many of our practices began with the players and me shoveling the latest snowfall off our court or scraping off a new layer of January ice. We couldn't do anything about those twenty-degree temperatures, however, or those stiff breezes blowing across that windy hilltop.

We stuck it out that way all winter long, and our games always meant more to us than to our opponents, because we got to play indoors. It was a luxury only we could appreciate. We were one team that was delighted to play nothing but road games.

Still, we won our division championship on our way to the quarter-finals, with that new team and no gym. The next year we went one better and made it to the semifinals. Our football team went undefeated again, and even the baseball team was beginning to win.

Our teams were going great guns, but I kept reminding myself I was at Saint Joseph's to help build young men through a successful athletic program, not the other way around. Coaches at every level have a tendency to lose sight of their purpose at times, especially after success arrives. They start to put the cart before the horse by working harder and harder to develop their teams, using their boys or girls to do it, gradually forgetting that their real purpose should be to develop the kids, using their teams to do it.

At an orphanage, it's never hard to remember the difference. You're aware all the time that your reason for being there is to help the kids. Maybe that's why I've never had to worry about losing sight of the real order of priorities. Maybe every coach should start his career in an orphanage.

One boy at Saint Joseph's was headed for big trouble when our paths crossed. The kid had two and a half strikes against him already. His mother put him in the orphanage because she had rejected him. She wanted no part of him, and he knew it. His father? Forget it: unseen, unknown, unheard from. As far as the kid was concerned, his father didn't exist—and for all we knew the boy was right.

The kid started stealing. Every time we turned around, the police were bringing him back to the place after catching him trying to steal something. I got him aside and put it to him in straight terms: "I hope you become the best athlete you can and later the best citizen you can instead of doing what you're doing now: trying to be the best thief you can."

Those words reached that kid. We started spending some time together. I took him to my house and he'd enjoy Mom's meals. He spent weekends with us. He became friends with my brother and sisters. He's still in Washington today and doing quite well and known to a lot of people. Anyone would be proud to call him their son. He was bound for a life of crime and jail, however, and maybe a lot worse, until someone gave him the greatest gift a parent can give a child—his time.

Another boy was placed in Saint Joseph's because his mother simply couldn't afford to keep him. His father had deserted them, and his mother had to give him up. It broke her heart, but there seemed no other way. When he reached high school age, the nuns at the orphanage didn't think he was ready for the academic challenges of a standard high school and were going to send him to a vocational school to learn a trade. There's nothing wrong with that, but I thought this boy had more potential.

I went to Johnny Ryall again and we worked out a solution. He could live at my apartment and Johnny would pay his tuition to go to Saint John's High School, the Catholic military school in Washington. We got him released from the orphanage and he came to live with me. We spent a lot of time at the Wootten home on Thornhill Road in Silver Spring with my parents and my brother and sisters. He stayed with me for two years. Then, in the kind of happy ending you always pray for, his mother remarried and once again could afford to keep him, so he returned to his mom and his new dad, finished his schooling and is doing well in Washington today as a sales executive —not a sales*man* but a sales *executive*.

In the years since, I've been best man at his wedding, godfather to his son, and his companion for many a round of golf. Johnny Ryall and I just knew he would make it.

The solid relationship and real affection which existed between the boys and me reached a level which could have been downright fatal, however, the night the brand-new heavyweight champion of the world came to Saint Joseph's.

He was Rocky Marciano, and he had won the title from Jersey Joe Walcott only a few nights before. Pete Haley, Sr., the founder of CYO sports in Washington, had talked him into coming out to the orphanage after a personal appearance downtown.

We had just finished reciting our evening rosary when the new champ arrived. He spent a long time with our kids, talking to them in our auditorium and telling them about boxing and his career, reminding them about leading the right kind of life and encouraging them to make a go of things despite their lives as orphans.

Then Marciano answered questions, as long and as graciously as you could imagine. For many of the boys in that audience, I was the only male figure in their lives, and some of our younger ones really weren't sure who this Marciano guy was, anyhow. One of them took it upon himself to stand up and ask, "Rocky, do you think you could beat Morgan?"

Marciano maintained his composure, looked me over, shook his head and said, "I don't really know. Boy, it would be a great fight. I'm a little bigger than he is, but it would be a terrific fight, no question about it."

The kid came back with, "I don't think you can. I think Morgan would kill you."

It gave me one claim to fame. I became the only man Rocky Marciano ever expressed any doubt about being able to beat. More than that, however, the incident told me something: I was reaching those boys.

An Unlikely Combination

1956: I came to DeMatha. For thirty-two hundred dollars a year, I was head football coach, head basketball coach, assistant baseball coach, athletic director, world history teacher five periods a day and the guy who called the numbers at Bingo every Tuesday night. The second year they told me they wanted me to work full time.

—MORGAN WOOTTEN

After two years, Morgan left Saint Joseph's—but not for DeMatha, not yet. The next step was Saint John's High School, working for Joe Gallagher, an unlikely move in many ways. After the experiences some of Joe Gallagher's athletes at Saint John's had had with Morgan Wootten in high school, you'd think hiring Wootten would have been the last thing Gallagher would have done.

Saint John's is a solid, no-nonsense Catholic military school, located then in downtown Washington and since moved to a green spread near the Maryland suburbs to the north. Even though he attended rival Gonzaga while in high school, Wootten continued to pal around with his grade school buddies, Tommy Clark and Dave Waldron, "Doonie" to his friends, both of them football stars at Saint John's. As a result, Morgan spent as much time with the "enemy" during that time as he did with his

16

Gonzaga classmates, and that's when he first ran across Joe Gallagher.

Gallagher, now a national coaching legend in his own right with nearly six hundred and fifty lifetime wins (an average of twenty wins a year for thirty-two years), was also football coach and athletic director of Saint John's, and he had rules about things like training and curfew which somehow interfered with the social habits of some of his ballplayers—and their good friend from Gonzaga.

There was the time in Newport, Rhode Island, for instance. Saint John's was in Newport for the Eastern States Catholic Invitational Basketball Tournament, led by their sensational star, Jack George, who would later go on to success at LaSalle and eight years in the NBA. Sixteen-year-old Morgan Wootten was there with his buddies, too, and presently adjourned with several players to George's room for a friendly game of chance with a deck of cards.

Just before the appointed hour for bed check, Morgan slipped a mattress off one of the beds and headed for the tub in the bathroom for a brief rest until the coach had finished making his nightly rounds. In a few minutes there came a rap, the door opened and there stood Coach Gallagher.

He surveyed the scene quickly, spotted the closed bathroom door and asked, "Jack, is there anybody else in here?"

"Oh, no, Coach, just me and Frank," George said, as he nodded toward his roommate, Frank Fannon.

Gallagher pointed to one of the beds and said innocently, "Hey, Jack, the hotel seems to have shortchanged you boys. One of your beds is missing its mattress."

No response.

The coach resumed: "I think I'll just have a little look in the bathroom here." He opened the door and there was Morgan, curled up on a mattress in the bathtub and wrapped in a sheet.

"You hadn't planned on spending the night, had you, Morgan?"

"No, sir, Coach. I was just getting a little rest before going back to my room."

Gallagher, a marine during World War II, threw the kid out. Or so he thought. Wootten slipped back in through a window and spent the night anyway, playing poker until dawn with Gallagher's most important players.

That wasn't the end of it, however. After the game broke up, his buddies slipped some breakfast back into the room for him and he sat down in the middle of one of the beds in his underwear to enjoy it, the Saint John's stars around him fully dressed because they had just come back from breakfast. That was how Brother Andrew found them.

Brother Andrew was one of the top-ranking members of the Saint John's administration, and he glared down at this kid in his skivvies and said, "You didn't spend the night in here, did you, Morgan?"

"No, Brother. I wouldn't do that."

Even the strongest of friendships have their limits, though, and this one had reached it right there. "Yes, he did, Brother," Jack George said with disgust. "And he took all our money."

The young intruder was excused in no uncertain terms once and for all—but he managed to get out with his night's earnings still in his pocket.

This was the teenager who, four years later, would be placing considerable emphasis on discipline and rules as a head coach himself. Before those days came, however, there were other escapades, one of which could have put an end to Wootten's career before it even started.

Tommy Clark was sitting in a barber shop in Silver Spring a couple of years later, getting his hair cut, when

Morgan came through the door for a trim. Before he could sit down, however, Tommy waylaid him. "Come on, Morgan, hurry up. We're going to Newport."

"How come?"

"Saint John's won last night so we'll be playing in the tournament up there in at least two more games. If we hustle, we can make the one tonight."

"How are we getting there?"

"In your car. Come on, man. Let's go."

That was all Morgan needed to hear, so off they went. This was back in the days when Washington to Rhode Island was an all-day endurance test along Route 1 and other highways long since forgotten in the mists of time. Before heading north, however, they received a prediction from Tommy's brother, Dave. He looked Morgan's seven-year-old Buick up and down and back and forth, then looked at the two adventurers standing there. "Don't wire me for money from the other side of Baltimore (only forty miles away) after you guys break down," he said. "That is, if you even make it to the other side of Baltimore."

The warning properly scoffed at, Dave retired and Tommy suggested they pick up a road map. Morgan, ever confident, said, "Man, we don't need a road map. I know the way. I made it there before, didn't I?"

So the two pointed the Buick north on Route 1 and worked their way through all the truck traffic and the gray industrialized landscape between Washington and New York, then picked up the Merritt Parkway above New York City for the stretch into New England. Morgan knew the way, all right, no question about it.

They continued on the Merritt Parkway—and on and on and on. Morgan had missed a turn. To be more precise, Morgan had forgotten a turn. When his mistake finally occurred to him, they were in the heart of downtown Eagleville, Connecticut—unknown miles and hours off their schedule.

They finally staggered into Newport at dawn, nearly twenty-four hours later, exhausted and almost broke. They ran into a local citizen in a coffee shop who apparently had been up all night too, but for a different reason. As he worked his way back to the real world of sobriety, the man asked, "Where you boys from?"

"Bangor, Maine. We're here for the tournament," they said, not wanting to embarrass Saint John's with their shabby appearance. Besides, Bangor did have a team in the tournament.

Maybe it was because he was a nice man, or maybe it was just because he was in an extra good mood from his night out on the town, but whatever the reason, their new acquaintance suddenly seemed to sprout the wings of an angel. He took them home and let them get some sleep, surrounded by priceless New England antiques.

The travelers were confident that things were going their way now, and by the time they had thanked their Samaritan, seen all the games they wanted and started back to Washington, they knew they had put together a successful trip after all.

But the trip wasn't over. Inevitably, as Dave had warned, they developed car trouble—just outside Baltimore. "If we have to pay somebody at a garage to get the car fixed," Morgan warned Tommy, "we'll have to call your brother, and after he finds out where we are ..." Fortunately, they never had to follow that thought to its conclusion, because with the proper diligence, they were able to fix the car themselves, and finally they limped back into Silver Spring late in the evening, exhausted and broke.

The next morning, rested, shaved and glad he had made the trip, even with all that happened, maybe even *because* of all that happened, Morgan bounded down the stairs of the Wootten home and out the front door—only to be greeted by the sight of three flat tires. That evening he asked the manager of the gas station he had managed to work his car to, "How bad were they?"

The manager stared at him in disbelief and slowly repeated the question: "How bad were they? . . . Friend, let me tell you about the best of the three first. Your *best* innertube had seven patches in it already."

They had just driven a thousand miles on three tires ready to blow at any moment. All that time, Morgan's car had been a disaster just waiting to happen. Morgan has been a strong believer in Saint Christopher ever since, and he doesn't care what anybody says.

He has another reason for remembering those Newport tournaments, as well . . .

When I got into coaching, I remember I would dream that some day I'd be able to take a team up there, the way Joe Gallagher had, and win the championship. My dream came true in 1962 when we won the title with a team headed by John Austin, who went on to play for Boston College, and then again the next year, this time with Brendan McCarthy, who made high school All-American for us in both football and basketball and then followed John to BC. The year after that, the tournament was discontinued. My dream had come true just in time.

Those earlier trips with my buddies on the Saint John's team helped form my long friendship with Joe Gallagher. Despite some of those escapades—and Joe always knew I was leading his athletes astray around a poker table—he came to a sports banquet I put on after my first year at Saint Joseph's, the first one they'd ever had there, and delivered one of the featured speeches.

Then the next year he asked me to help him. He needed

a junior varsity coach for both football and basketball, and I realized it was time for me to move on. After making sure the kids would be taken care of and the sports program would be continued after I left, I took Joe up on his offer and began the kind of career I still pursue today: history teacher and coach, the same combination Joe also has followed all of his professional life. To this day, you can't reach either one of us until after lunch and for the same reason: We're both in the classroom all morning, Joe teaching American history and me world history.

I spent one season at Saint John's and it wasn't long before other avenues opened up. In my second season, a relatively new school named DeMatha over in Hyattsville in Prince George's County came looking for a basketball coach.

It's funny how things work out. Father Louis, DeMatha's president, offered me the job, and that's how I got started there, right? Wrong. I turned the job down. I thought I'd be taking on too much after only one year in the classroom by also becoming the head coach at a school. I thanked him for the compliment, but said no thanks.

The next year, Father Louis showed up again, and this time I was ready. I jumped at the opportunity, satisfied by now that I could handle the combined load. My relationship with DeMatha began in the fall of 1956—I was twenty-four years old—and apparently we were made for each other, because after nearly a quarter of a century, we're still together.

On that September morning in 1956, when Morgan Wootten arrived on the DeMatha grounds, the coach wasn't the only one who was young and ambitious. The school was, too. It sat, as it does now, one block off the industrial/commercial strip of Route 1 in Hyattsville, a red two-story building, its two long wings joined at a right angle. A few feet away is the monastery which houses the priests and brothers of the Immaculate Heart of Mary Province of the Order of the Most Holy Trinity.

DeMatha had opened its doors only ten years before, the year Morgan was starting the tenth grade. The founding fathers had named their school in honor of Saint John DeMatha, the young French priest who had established the Trinitarians eight hundred years ago. As their school mascot, they had chosen the stag, an animal found in the forest of Cerfoid in France, where John DeMatha had spent long periods of time in prayer and meditation.

The original goal of the new DeMatha Catholic High School was to provide a high school education for young men interested in preparing for the priesthood in the Order of the Most Holy Trinity. The word soon got around, however, that it was a good school, and before long the priests and brothers found themselves running a full-fledged high school with an enrollment which has grown from eighteen boys in 1946 to nearly nine hundred today. It is involved in a curriculum that includes ninety-five different courses. Most of the students come from the area around the school in Prince George's County, but a few are drawn from adjacent Montgomery County and more distant parts of Washington, and several boys even come from outside the United States.

The basketball team that represents DeMatha is recognized everywhere now as a national, even international, powerhouse, the home of All-Americans and Olympic stars. Back in September 1956, however, things were a bit different.

The quote at the beginning of this chapter really is true and says it all. I was a coach nobody had ever heard of arriving at a school nobody had ever heard of. The DeMatha Stags were a doormat if any team ever was. The school had just dropped out of the Catholic League because it was getting consistently clobbered. To take one example, the Stags had just lost to Saint John's in football, 54–0. Everybody did that to them, and in every sport, not just football.

Father Louis had had enough of that business when he came to me the second time. "There's no reason for us to be taking this kind of a beating," he said. "I want a young man who can come in here and develop a winning program and grow with it." That's exactly what I was hoping he would say.

The morning I began at DeMatha, its enrollment was well under two hundred students for four grades, and I had one coach to help me—Buck Offutt. Together we coached every team in every sport at the freshman, junior varsity and varsity levels. Equipment? It was either poor or nonexistent. But that didn't make any difference: There wasn't any place to keep it anyway.

People have often asked me what was the first thing I did on arriving at DeMatha. I always answer by telling them the first *two* things I did. First, I held a meeting for any boy who was interested in playing any sport at DeMatha in that 1956/57 school year. About fifty of them showed up. It didn't take long to tell them why I had called the meeting.

I gave it to them straight: "Fellas, things are going to change. I know how bad DeMatha's teams have been during these last few years, but that's over with. We're going to win at DeMatha and we're going to build a *tradition* of winning. Starting right now. If you want to climb aboard

24

this bandwagon, we'd love to have you, and I can tell you right now you're going to have a lot of fun and win a lot of games.

"But let me tell you how we're going to do it. We're going to outwork every team we ever play. We're going to show up on time for every practice, and work harder than our opposing teams are working in their practices and make all the sacrifices it takes, and then get out there on the field and outwork them during the game, too. All this losing stuff is finished as of now. With a lot of hard work and discipline and dedication, people are going to hear about us and respect us, because DeMatha will be a winner."

It wasn't just a pep talk, or a con job. I meant every word of it. I really believed it. Here I was arriving to coach a chronic loser and I had more confidence than other coaches who had championship teams every year. I was inheriting lousy teams, a program that couldn't even be called a program and equipment that looked like somebody's idea of a cruel joke. But I never doubted for one minute that we would win.

I knew what kind of athletes I wanted, the same kind I still want today. I'm old-fashioned enough—some say corny—to find inspiration in poems and sayings by people I respect, successful people—winners. Some are at the beginning of the chapters of this book. I quote my favorites to my teams all the time because all of us can learn so much from these winners. I hand out copies of these messages to my teams, and to all the boys and girls who attend the Metropolitan Basketball Camp and soccer camp which Joe Gallagher and I conduct each summer in Washington. One of my favorites is "Boys Wanted," by Douglas Mac-

Arthur, and it tells of the kind of athlete I wanted then and still want now, the kind any good coach is always looking for:

> Wanted: Boys who'll bide their time,
> And wait the hills of life to climb,
> Boys out of school who do not seek
> A grown man's wages in a week,
> And will not sell the future years
> For some small gain which now appears;
> Bright, eager boys who want to learn
> And work for more than what they earn.
>
> Boys wanted of a rugged stock
> Who will not daily watch the clock;
> Ambitious boys, alert to see
> Wherever they can useful be;
> Boys who are not inclined to shirk
> But put their hearts into their work
> And go to tasks which must be done
> As though it were their greatest fun.
>
> Boys wanted—not the flabby kind
> That seek some easy post to find
> Not careless boys who think the boss
> Is rich enough to suffer loss
> But boys who think and work and train
> For that promotion they may gain
> And for that job should prepare—
> Such boys are wanted everywhere.

I was absolutely certain the boys would respond. I had seen proof of that in my work at Saint Joseph's and Saint

John's, and I saw the first signs of success early at DeMatha. We played .500 football that fall, something nobody dreamed possible. We topped that in basketball by winning our division championship. Just to show we were no fluke, we went out and won the baseball championship, too. That baseball title sounds as if I had learned an awful lot about that sport since my 0–16 start at Saint Joseph's, but there was an easy explanation: Buck Offutt was De-Matha's baseball coach. I was only his assistant.

One of the things that helped us considerably in basketball was the presence of Ernie Cage. Ernie was a junior, destined to make All-Metropolitan and become a starter at Mount Saint Mary's. With him, we won twenty games and lost only six. Twenty and six! Everyone was delighted, and I was so thrilled for the boys, after they had suffered so much in previous seasons, that I could hardly stand the fun and excitement myself. We even upset the defending champions, Gonzaga. Against Joe Gallagher and my old friends at Saint John's, the experiences were mixed. In our first game, Cage missed his ride and didn't arrive until the second quarter—and they beat us by forty points. The next time, he got there on time and we beat *them* by two points.

DeMatha wasn't used to getting invited to postseason tournaments, but it happened right off the bat that first year when we got to participate in the Knights of Columbus tournament at the University of Maryland. We lost by one point to Saint Francis of New York when Ernie's shot at the buzzer rimmed the basket and dropped out. That didn't make us fold our hands in dejection, however, and creep off into the night. Not at all, we were thrilled. We knew then we could play this game. We were on our way.

I said I did *two* things that first day at DeMatha. The first was the meeting. The second was also a key factor in our quick success, but it surprises everyone. I took a vacation. For two weeks, Buck Offutt and I went up to Cape May, New Jersey, lounged around on the beach, and did a lot of talking, went over a lot of papers on coaching and got to know each other well enough to begin to feel comfortable working with each other. If it was just going to be the two of us carrying the whole athletic load, I thought we'd better learn how we fit together. Two weeks off by ourselves in a relaxed atmosphere with no interruptions seemed to me the best way to go about it. I'd recommend it to any coach or any other executive walking into a strange new program.

Thanks to Buck, I even got "promoted" to athletic director my first year there. Buck was my assistant in football and basketball, but I was his in baseball. After we won the baseball championship, the Archdiocese newspaper, the *Catholic Standard*, ran a picture of our team, identifying Buck correctly as the baseball coach, but then I guess they couldn't figure out what I was doing there. I certainly couldn't be assistant to a guy who was my assistant in every other sport, so they identified me as the athletic director. That was the first time anyone had ever called me that, but having been appointed in the newspaper caption, I've been the athletic director ever since—and DeMatha has never felt the need to make it any more official than that.

Buck has done all right, too. Today he is Charles Offutt, Ed.D., a highly respected member of the DeMatha faculty, and chairman of our English department. And, all these years after those two weeks at Cape May, he's still my friend.

I never set any timetable for success during my early days at DeMatha. There are other ways to achieve it and a timetable doesn't help. The only things that help are hard work, imagination and perseverance—not letting anything discourage or distract you. These are the elements you must have if you are to make immediate progress toward a successful program:

1. You must have good people.
2. You must build the support of your faculty and administration.
3. You must develop the support of your community —parents, the school's neighbors, local merchants and civic leaders.

The requirement for good people is right at the top of the list. Without them, you'll never make it. You simply must have good athletes and assistant coaches, and by "good athletes," I don't mean just talented ballplayers, I mean people who will work hard, get good grades in school, behave themselves away from school, maintain a proper team attitude and strive to develop their talents to the maximum.

The high school level is different from any level they've played on before. Before, the emphasis should have been on developing rather than winning. By the time the kids reach high school, however, they are only one step away either from college or from moving into the outside world. In either case, that next step will be into a highly competitive situation, so it is our obligation to prepare them to survive in that environment. For that reason, the young men we look for in our basketball program are competitors, young men not afraid of paying the price, who actually welcome the opportunity. That first year, and ever since, we have told our players that if they are afraid of competing now, they'll never make it in later life, not in a society which places such great emphasis on competition. It's seldom a problem for us, however. The kind of kid we want is usually the kind of kid that's drawn to DeMatha in the first place.

That first year at DeMatha, I also made it clear that there was a great deal of hard work involved in what we were going to be doing. I believe that basketball should be fun, but my players must understand that worthwhile things in life do not come easily. Winning is fun, but winning requires work. There is no substitute for it, as I've learned time and time again over the years.

I don't just mean hard work in athletics. In seeking and developing the DeMatha athlete, I always emphasize that we don't want the player who excels only on the playing field, we want the young man who excels in the classroom as well. We want the *student-athlete*, and we are not the only ones. More and more, college coaches are looking for the same thing. Coaches cannot afford to use up their limited number of athletic scholarships and invest their funds and time in a ballplayer who will be declared scholastically ineligible halfway through the season. Scouts and coaches come into my office in such numbers during and after the basketball season that I have thought of putting up a revolving door, and they all tell me the same thing these days: "Give me a senior who has been a good student at DeMatha, not just Cs, but As and

Bs, a guy who has been on your honor roll. That's the kind of player I'm looking for, so I know he'll be playing when I need him."

From our standpoint, there is another reason for looking for the excellent student as well. A true competitor will do his best in everything he attempts. As a result, his excellence in the classroom will have a great deal to do with his excellence on the basketball court. By the same token, the student who quits in the classroom will also quit on the court. We don't want that kind of person. The term is not just athlete but student-athlete, and it's no accident that student comes first.

We tell our players that we want people who will lead the parade, not those who are satisfied just to march in it. This is important because from the time an athlete puts on a uniform until he retires, and sometimes for years later, he is looked up to for leadership and guidance. He must be able to accept that responsibility for being a leader.

I summarize it for our players by telling them at the beginning of the season, "The players who make the team at DeMatha are competitors both in the classroom and on the basketball court, they are student-athletes, they are leaders in the school, they are young men who are dedicated, they are willing to discipline themselves, they are willing to make sacrifices, they are willing to work and they are willing to pay the price. THEY ARE UNIQUE."

One other thing that is very important: It is my own belief that you have to have a goal in life, maybe more than one, maybe one that changes from time to time depending on your situation, but a goal nevertheless. You run the risk of stepping into a trap, however, if you make that goal a numerical one, if you say, "I want us to win twenty games in our first year" (though we did), or, "I want to be making X dollars a year by the time I'm forty."

Sometimes that works, but sometimes it doesn't. In the case of a coach, too many things can happen—injuries, for instance. If you lose your star and don't win those twenty games, does that mean you were not successful? Maybe you only won twelve games, but under the circumstances those twelve wins might have meant a successful season.

If you set numerical goals, *not* reaching them implies that you failed, and that's not necessarily the case. Here's another example, a real one. I think you could argue that my first baseball year at Saint Joseph's was a success. A successful season when I didn't win a game? And I lost sixteen? Sure. Those boys had fun, learned many valuable lessons from their adversity—and asked me to come back. Under the conditions which surrounded that team, I'd say that was a successful season.

A friend of mine coached kids' football and baseball when his boy, who is now in high school, was younger. Together they worked their way up from the second grade through the ninth grade, and at the beginning of every season, he would tell his players not to get hung up on the team's won-lost record. At their age, he would say, only three things would tell them if they'd had a 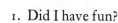 successful season:

1. Did I have fun?
2. Did I learn?
3. Did I improve?

"If you can answer yes to all three of those questions

when it's all over," he'd say, "then you've had a successful season, and our won-lost record won't make any difference. At your age, you can have a good season even if you never win a game. But if you haven't gotten to play or learn or improve, it won't have been successful even if the team went undefeated."

And with that attitude, he won four championships in six seasons of football and baseball.

My friend, of course, was working with elementary school, and later junior high school, boys. Things are a bit different at the high school level, as any high school coach will tell you, because of the emphasis on competition and winning. I agree with that emphasis—as I've said, we have to prepare students to be able to compete in life. We have to show them how to win—and how to overcome defeat when they lose, because losing is also a part of life, and learning how to survive it and come back is essential if you are to win again.

However, for a coach to say he can't be a success if his team doesn't win a specific number of games in the coming season, or win the championship within three years, or whatever, is a mistake. It's setting a goal which may not be attainable and not only does the players, but the coach, an injustice because it's a meaningless standard.

Finally, there is one more essential ingredient for building a winning program, or a winning anything. During World War II, when Winston Churchill was England's prime minister, he was invited to speak at the Harrow School to tell them how to succeed in life and to give the formula which had enabled him to rise to his position as wartime leader of a great nation. He went to the lectern and told his audience of boys:

"Never give in! Never give in! Never, never, never, never—in nothing great or small, large or petty—never give in, except to convictions of honor and good sense."

Then he sat down.

That was the end of his speech. He had said it all. You can't make it in life unless you stick to your guns through everything imaginable, but if you do, success can be yours. That's what I tell my students in world history and my students in basketball. I recommend it to everyone—students, coaches, parents and anyone else—as a key to success.

To my fellow coaches, specifically, that's the formula for starting a winning program: Get good assistants and good student-athletes, get the support of your faculty and administration, get the support of your community—and never give in.

To Be the Best:
Preparing for Power Memorial

Genius is 1 percent inspiration, and 99 percent perspiration.

—THOMAS ALVA EDISON

The effective use of those two ingredients, even if his percentages were different from Edison's, brought success to Morgan Wootten early and consistently at DeMatha. For those who thought his twenty wins at a chronic loser of a school was a fluke, he had an answer: another twenty wins in his second year, and every year since, topped off by his 1977/78 national championship team's record of 27–0.

There have been other high points, other milestones of achievement—division championships, Metropolitan Washington championships, national Catholic championships, tournament championships—more than sixty in all. The highest point, however, even today, occurred on the night of January 30, 1965. On that date, the page-one banner headline of the Washington *Daily News* read:

35

NATION'S FINEST
12,000 to See New York's Power Memorial & DeMatha Here Tonight

Placed prominently below were two rows of pictures —Power Memorial's Jack Donohue and his five starters and Wootten and his five—and underneath that an array of facts and figures: the full name, uniform number, height, weight, year in school and position of the two starting lineups. The information ran to the bottom of page one and across the bottom ran one more line:

See Preview Story, Cartoon, Complete Rosters &
Kiernan's Corner on Page 17

On a day when Lyndon Johnson and Hubert Humphrey were just beginning their four-year terms, when the war was raging in Vietnam and all manner of events were happening in the nation and around the world, the number-one story, the *only* story, on page one was a high school basketball game.

Why all the excitement? Simply, this: The Panthers of New York's Power Memorial Academy were undefeated, riding the crest of a phenomenal seventy-one-game winning streak, and boasting the talents of the equally phenomenal high school superstar, Lew Alcindor (now Kareem Abdul-Jabbar). It would be the greatest challenge ever for the DeMatha Stags, the former losers, the one-time doormats, who had not only risen to national respect, but were themselves undefeated, with seventeen wins for the season and a winning streak of twenty-nine games.

On the day of the game, 12,500 people filled Cole Field House at the University of Maryland (Cole has since been expanded to accommodate 14,500). All the Washington papers were there . . . all the Washington radio and television stations . . . *Time* magazine . . . *News-*

week . . . CBS . . . NBC. It was, and in the opinion of most people, still is, the greatest high school basketball game ever played.

But it almost never happened. The problem started a long time before the 1965 classic, a year earlier, in fact, when Power and DeMatha were scheduled to play their first game ever against each other. Father Louis, Dematha's moderator, had serious doubts about the game, and called Morgan Wootten into his office.

I was on the spot. Father Louis laid it out for me. He knew I had agreed to pay Power's traveling expenses—train, room and board—about three thousand dollars. "Morgan," he said, "we're going to lose our shirts on this game." He said we had to move it from Maryland University to Catholic University in Washington. We'd save a lot of rent money. The only problem was we'd also lose close to ten thousand spectators, since Catholic had a smaller gym.

I was opposed to the whole idea. DeMatha was trying to make a national name for itself and we were so close—this was no time to pull up scared. I had scheduled the game because of Power's tremendous national reputation and because every coach knew all about Lew Alcindor. We had proven in the past few years that we could beat the good teams, not just in our county or our metropolitan area, but in the whole East. We were playing—and with success—against the best teams in Washington, Baltimore, Philadelphia and New York and making believers everywhere we went. Now I wanted to take on the biggest national name around. I wanted to show that we could beat the best, and to do that you had to *play* the best. That's why I had scheduled our meeting in 1964, and that's why I wasn't going to move it to a small gym. I wanted as many witnesses as possible.

Father Louis made it clear that he didn't see it that way. I knew all I needed was a little time, to raise some money, so I said, "Father, just give me one day." He gave it to me, but was plainly skeptical. "I'll be happy if we can just cut our losses to five hundred or a thousand dollars," he said.

This was a job for Rodney Breedlove. Rod and I had gone to the University of Maryland together where he had been a football star, following a great high school career in Cumberland, Maryland. We became great buddies at Maryland and still are. He was an usher at my wedding, traveled with us on our road games and later we formed the Washington Redskins basketball team together.

In those years, though, Rod was playing football for the Redskins, not basketball, and was their standout linebacker, good enough to make All-Pro. I got him on the phone. "How would you like to get involved in a business venture with me?" We had a quick meeting later that day during which I gave him the details and told him we could buy the game ourselves and be its sponsors. All it would take would be three thousand dollars each. He'd never miss it from that fat pro football salary, I said, and as for me, I'd wipe out my savings account and mortgage everything if necessary, but I just knew we could turn a comfortable profit if we kept that game in front of twelve thousand fans instead of three thousand.

Rod asked the decisive question. "Will the game go?"

"It can't miss."

We had a deal. Now all I had to do was convince Father Louis to let us do it, then figure out where I was going to get three thousand dollars for my half of the deal. But first things first.

I went back to Father Louis the next day, well within my deadline of twenty-four hours, and gave him the good news. "Father, I have a sponsor."

"Who is it?"

"Rodney Breedlove and a friend."

Father Louis always wanted all the information, not just most of it, and he always asked the right questions to get it.

"Who's his friend?"

"Me."

He didn't hesitate, never even batted an eyelash. "Morgan, if you think it's that good a deal, then I'm not about to let you buy the game. It's still DeMatha's game, and we're still playing it at Maryland."

Which was exactly what happened—and of course the place did sell out, all 12,500 seats of it. On the night of the game, tickets which had cost two dollars were being scalped for twenty-five dollars. DeMatha's profit—profit, mind you—which would have gone to Rod and me if Father Louis hadn't been so alert, was twenty thousand dollars.

We didn't win the game; we lost by three in the last minute, but we gave them everything they could handle. Now the world knew we belonged right up there with anybody, and it just made me hungry for more. Now that we had proved we could play evenly with the best teams in the country, we had to prove we could beat them. Power's coach, Jack Donohue, and I agreed immediately to play again in 1965 at Cole Field House.

I don't think anyone, including coaches, should become

obsessed with winning a game, and I deliberately try to avoid making that mistake. You can get so hopped up that as a result you make life miserable for yourself and for everyone else around you at home and at work; you reduce your day-to-day effectiveness as you point ahead only to "The Big One," and you even run the risk of losing control and making the mistakes that could cost you that big game. For all these reasons, coaches—for that matter, professionals in any field—must maintain their equilibrium or they'll blow more than the game.

Avoiding that obsession doesn't mean you can't work hard and long to achieve your goal, though, and that's what we did, starting right after our 1964 loss to Power. It wasn't just a case of wanting a big win against a big name. So many other things would follow a win over Power. We'd show that our performance against them, which had stunned everyone except ourselves, was no mere flash in the pan, that DeMatha had as much claim to national basketball respect as any other school in the United States. We wanted to beat the best to be the best—and after that, we wanted to keep on being the best, to build a permanent basketball dynasty, so that when people thought of high school basketball supremacy, they would think of DeMatha.

One of the first results of all this planning was that we immediately became Power's biggest boosters. We wanted them undefeated when we met them the following year, so that there would be no question after we won that we *had* beaten the best.

Another result was that I immediately installed some new procedures for myself. You really can learn from your mistakes. After the game, two of my seniors, Brendan

McCarthy, a football and basketball All-American who would later go on to play for the Denver Broncos, and Joe Kennedy, who had a career at Duke and in the NBA ahead of him, came to see me. I've always encouraged my players and my coaches to talk frankly to me when they have an idea or a complaint. I've never claimed to be a genius and I never made any claims to be infallible on the subject of basketball. I need as much help as anyone else, and they had come to give me some. One of our problems, they told me, was that I had not had enough time for coaching before the game. I had been so busy selling tickets around town, making personal appearances to promote the game, lining up transportation and other arrangements for the visitors, and doing a million other things, that I had spread myself too thin.

Brendan would say later about the 1964 game: "I won't say Morgan was uptight, but I sneezed one day and he threw me out of practice."

They were absolutely right (and two months later, incidentally, both of them served as altar boys at my wedding). I had tried to do everything myself, and I swore that next year I would concentrate on what counted most. As it turned out, it was an easy promise to keep. The first game had been such a box-office smash that, like magic, promotion committees, ticket distribution committees and all sorts of volunteers appeared on the scene to take care of the other things, and all I had to do was coach.

My coaches and I immediately started looking ahead to 1965, while at the same time taking care to shield our players from the pressures and preoccupations that come from working too far ahead of time. Coaches make that mistake all the way from the CYO to the NBA, from Little League to the World Series or the Super Bowl, and it's one we have always remained aware of and avoided. The coaches started working right away. We got the films back, looked at them what seemed a million times, then proceeded to break down and analyze what we had done and they had done, what worked for each team and what didn't, and countless other factors. The players were not involved with any of this, however. We completed the rest of our schedule with them, held our spring meeting in May, 1965, to tell candidates for the next season what they should work on over the summer, held our September meeting to tell the boys what to do until practice began, started practice in November, everything as usual—all without hammering away about the Power return match. That would have been fatal to our hopes.

Meanwhile, after all those viewings of the 1964 game film, the coaches had made a key decision: We decided to reverse our game strategy. The first time, we had decided to let Lew Alcindor get his twenty-six or twenty-eight points a game with his seven-foot height around the basket. The plan had been to beat Power by shutting down everybody else—one guy couldn't beat us by himself, could he? Well, one guy *did:* Lew scored thirty-eight points. Consequently, this time we decided to go after him, to do everything we could to shut him off and deny him the ball. I was determined that if we were going to lose to Power twice, at least we weren't going to do it the same way.

I have followed that strategy of shutting off the other team's big man ever since. If a team is going to beat us, they'll have to do it from the outside, and that usually doesn't happen. The inside game wins almost every time because the shots are high-percentage shots. The other team can take those eighteen-footers all night, and may beat us occasionally, but, nine times out of ten, if we're able to take the inside game away, then we'll win—and so will any coach who tries it.

We never prepared for Power by name until the week of the game. At those May and September meetings I had deliberately warned our boys not to get so blinded by that game waiting for us on our '65 schedule that they found themselves getting knocked off by a lesser team before then. "Fellas," I said, "I know it's a cliché, but we're going to play this season one game at a time. By the time we get to that night on the schedule, we want it to be a national high school event, and for that to happen both teams will have to stay undefeated. There's nothing that teams like Carroll, Saint John's or Gonzaga would like better than to catch us looking past them to our game with Power. If that's going to be the dream game that everybody says it is, you're going to have to do your part."

I brought it up only one more time. I always let my players make their own rules for the season—a process I'll discuss in a later chapter—and while we were going over the rules for this season, I made sure to point out the Power game. "Before you vote on your rules for this year," I said, "remember you're going to be playing before 12,500 people at the University of Maryland on January 31 against Power and you're going to want to be ready and in the absolutely finest physical condition possible."

Then we never mentioned Power again as we played our schedule and won our way through December and January. That doesn't mean we weren't getting the team

ready. Far from it. We were careful how we did it, however. We worked on new drills without telling our players
the drills were for use against Power. We just told them
near the end of a practice that we had some time left, so
let's work a little on this or that. We didn't lie to them.
We just didn't tell them those drills were for Power, and
they didn't ask. For instance, we worked on double blocking a big man under his offensive board. We had noticed
in the Power films that the offensive guard hung back to
protect against the opponent's fast break, instead of staying
near the board, so we realized we could afford to put a
second player on the big man. This way Power, probably
Lew, would only get one shot. His seven-foot advantage
would be taken right away from him.

All the special drills we worked on then were things
that would be helpful in any game, but especially useful
in the Power game—and all the time we made sure that
everything appeared normal, that we were concentrating in
each practice on the *next* opponent, not Power. It was
working. We kept winning game after game, until by
the time we met Power, it was twenty-nine straight, without even a close call. The question was, would the strategy
work in the big game itself?

Archbishop Carroll was our last game before Power,
and I had scheduled a whole week off afterward to give us
plenty of time to get ready. We practiced only once at
Cole Field House, to get the feel of Maryland's court
again. Our practices at DeMatha were packed, but that
was good because it got our guys used to a lot of crowd
noise. I've always allowed our practices to be open, to
everybody except the next opponent. Other teams on our
schedule come in and watch us; college scouts are always

in there; other DeMatha students come by: That's no problem. They're always welcome at my practice—and that week, everybody was taking advantage of the policy.

We spent a lot of time that week on our post defense, on double blocking and blocking out, keeping the ball away from the center, and doubling up on the opponent's guard, who was a good ball handler. We also worked on the medium-range jump shot for ourselves: bringing the ball upcourt as quickly as we could, then pulling up at the foul line for the twelve-to-fifteen footer. We worked on our full-court press, too, and on our zone defense. Our coaches wanted a backup plan in case our own big man, Sid Catlett—our power forward—and Bob Whitmore—our star center—got into early foul trouble. Whit had fouled out in the '64 game, and we wanted to be ready for that possibility this time with a zone we could turn to in an emergency.

We also worked on a little trick which Mickey Wiles made possible. Mickey was a star guard (and our quarterback in football) who would soon return to that same floor to play basketball for the University of Maryland. Watching Power's films, Mickey had alertly spotted a habit of Alcindor's. After getting a rebound, Lew would put his head down and start to run down the floor to his spot in Power's offense, barely aware of what was in front of him. So Mickey decided to trick him. During the game itself, Mickey would slide right in front of Alcindor while Lew had his head down with the rebound. Lew would never be looking—and would bang right into him. When you're seven feet two inches, and you hit the deck, you go down in sections, and that's the way you get up. Meanwhile, the Panthers would be downcourt trying to get something set up without their star center. It worked four or five times that night.

At our first practice of the week, I could see the first signs of nervousness. It wasn't surprising because by now the whole town was talking about THE GAME, and we weren't the only ones talking. It was a big story all week long in New York, too: two metropolitan areas of twelve million people talking about a high school basketball game. It had been sold out ten days in advance.

When I detected those first signs of jitters, however, I knew I had to get at them right away, so I assembled the guys early in that first practice and told them, "Look, fellas, we don't have to be uptight about this game because there's no way we can lose. If we get beaten, we were supposed to get beaten, so nobody's going to be down on us for it. We're not *going* to lose—we're going to win—but whatever happens, we want to be able to say we put in a lot of hard work and we had a lot of fun in this week's practices. We're in an enviable position, so let's have a ball this week. Work hard, but have a ball."

The result was one of the loosest weeks of practice we've ever had. We stuck to our regular time: two hours, no more no less. We were relaxed, we had fun and we worked hard. We were as thorough as possible. We knew what was within our reach: an opportunity to establish ourselves at a level that might never come our way again, certainly not with the kind of media exposure this game was getting. With a minute and a half left in our first Power game, the public address announcer had said during a timeout, "Ladies and gentlemen, regardless of who wins this game, I think we agree that we're watching the two finest high school teams in America here tonight." The crowd had responded with a standing ovation. That's what everyone was expecting in '65.

We covered everything we could think of, and then kept trying to think of more. Out of this constant searching came a unique wrinkle which I'm convinced helped us in that game. In addition to stopping Lew from getting too many points or rebounds, we had to keep him from blocking too many of our shots. In a high school game, a seven-foot-two-inch center can shut down almost everyone's offense, and we didn't want him doing that to us.

I was talking about it one day to John Moylan, a member of our faculty then and our principal now. I told him I was determined to find a way in practice to get our guys used to shooting over that giant and his long arms up in the air, even if it meant stationing Sid Catlett under the basket on a ladder and just having our guys shoot over him until they were able to make their shots. John came up with an even better idea. "Why not use my tennis racket?" It made a lot more sense: With a tennis racket, Sid could move around, which Alcindor certainly would be doing, instead of having to stay in one spot while we practiced shooting over him. As a result, Sid, who would later star at Notre Dame, spent a lot of time all week—all six feet eight inches of him—under the basket with John Moylan's racket high over his head, with orders from me to block every shot he could. With all that height and his long arms and the tennis racket to top it off, he looked like the Washington Monument in a DeMatha uniform. By the time he added his jumping ability, he was scraping the rafters. But it worked. Our players became accustomed to putting more arch on their shots, and by the time the game rolled around, a seven-foot shot-blocker was al-

47

most easy—unless he had a tennis racket, too.

Let me stop for a moment here and discuss another subject I am often asked about. How do you prepare a team for such a big game? How do you overcome the jitters? How can you cover all the technical questions, the Xs and Os, while also coping with the emotional challenges?

For that game, and for every big game since, I have followed several basic rules for myself as coach, and I think they are essential for any coach. Taken out of their athletic context, they can apply to executives or people in positions of responsibility in any field. Anyone with leadership responsibilities faces a "big game" of some nature from time to time. The basic rules I have set for myself when such challenges arise are these:

1. The coach must project a feeling of total confidence in his team's ability to win this game. If he doesn't, the players are going to sense it. They'll know it, and then they'll know they are in big trouble—because their coach is scared. If the coach is not confident, the players aren't. If the coach is nervous, the players are nervous. The atmosphere has to be relaxed, and the coach's every word and deed must tell his players, "We're going to beat this team, and here's how we're going to do it."

2. I never talk much about the other team. I talk instead about what *we're* going to do: *We're* going to dominate the defensive boards so they get only one shot, *we're* going to push the ball down the sideline, *we're* going to deny their big man the ball. I never build up the other team because my players will believe me. If I'm a good salesman, and I think I am, and if I have the respect of my team, and I think I do, then if I build up the other

team, I might build them up too big, which is a common mistake among coaches. I want to build up what *we're* going to do and have them believe me, and, thank the Good Lord, in most cases that's what we've wound up doing.

3. Be yourself. Often a young coach imitates another, trying to be an Auerbach, a Wooden, a Dean Smith or a Digger Phelps. That doesn't work. The kids will spot that a mile away. You have to remain yourself, *especially* preparing for a big game. Don't try to copy someone else's style. I always quote Polonius's advice from *Hamlet* to our players, and it's advice for coaches, too:

> Neither a borrower, nor a lender be,
> For loan oft loses both itself and friend,
> And borrowing dulls the edge of husbandry.
> This above all, to thine own self be true
> And it must follow, as night the day,
> Thou canst not then be false to any man.

In order to be himself, however, a coach has to have a good self-image, as do players. I tell everyone at DeMatha, "All of you should have a great image of yourselves because God made you and God doesn't make junk." People sometimes wish they were handsomer or taller or a better athlete or a better this or that. That's baloney. All beauty comes from within. That's why you can be justified feeling good about yourself.

I can remember, as a kid in Silver Spring, wishing I were a better athlete so I could be better at sports and more popular with my friends, like my best friend, Dave Waldron—"Doonie"—was. Unlike me, Doonie had everything: great athletic ability, good looks, everything a kid that age could ask for. Then it dawned on me: "If he and I are each other's best friend, and he sees that much in me, then I must have something going for me." It was my first awareness that people often shortchange themselves when it comes to their self-images.

4. Don't put in any major changes before your big game. One of the most foolish things a coach can do is to install a new offense or put in a new defense. You can work in a few changes, as we did, maybe an option off a play you already have, or some wrinkles which you can tell your team are "just to keep things interesting"—but nothing major. If you throw in some big new thing, your players will pick up your insecurity immediately and say to themselves, and maybe even to each other, "Coach doesn't have enough confidence in us. He thinks they're too tough for us." You can't win your big game with major changes. You have to do it with what you do best—and with salesmanship.

I love to find out that a team we're playing soon is altering its game for us. That tells me they think what they usually do won't work against us. When I hear that, I always feel like saying a short prayer of thanks because I know we'll win that game.

The day finally came. We were ready. I just knew it. I would have bet my life on it. Our knees weren't knocking in fear of anyone. Our players displayed total confidence —not in any conceited or arrogant way, because I won't allow that—but composed, mature. We were ready.

There was no escaping the fever. All the Washington papers were headlining the game. It was on every newscast on radio and television starting the night before and running all that day. My phones at home and at school were jumping off the hook with requests from reporters for telephone interviews and friends calling at the last minute to wish us luck—or ask for tickets. As soon as I put the phone down, it would ring again. It was impossible to get anything done.

I had to be careful that our athletes didn't get swallowed up in all this and lose their composure. We had to stay loose. I couldn't help noticing a definite contrast in team behavior when we hosted the Power team, its coaches and faculty members at a midafternoon luncheon in the DeMatha cafeteria. Their guys were quiet. Ours were relaxed and talking, sometimes even laughing. Not even the sight of Lew Alcindor bothered them when, as Bob Whitmore told people later, "At the pregame meal, the priest asked us to rise and say grace and Lew stood up— and up and up and up." When I took the team for a walk after the meal, I could still see it. They were still loose. So far, so good.

Meanwhile, unknown to me, the New York papers had run a couple of stories that week saying, in effect, "Knowledgeable sources are saying that Power's seventy-one-game winning streak could be nearing an end." Maybe that's why their players looked so tight at the luncheon.

When I entered the dressing room at Cole Field House that night, I saw nothing unusual. There was no phony screaming or hollering, which is a good sign, because my players are generally pretty quiet in the dressing room. There's no rock-and-roll music from somebody's portable stereo. Many teams have pop music blaring in their dressing rooms, but we don't. Our players have never requested it, so we've never done it. There was no clowning around because there never is before a game in the DeMatha dressing room. Players were doing what they always do: mentally reviewing their individual and team responsibilities for the night as they slipped on their red, white and blue uniforms and laced up their sneakers.

I always leave them alone in the dressing room until only a few minutes before game time. It's their dressing room and I don't intrude on them and their privacy until just before we're ready to take the floor. I did the same that night, then gave them a talk of only a few minutes. I avoid long talks before the game or at the half. Five minutes is enough: just a few basic reminders, then some motivation, with more emphasis on motivation than on the Xs and Os. I followed the same routine that night, still making sure to obey one of my cardinal rules for a big game: no major changes. Keep it business as usual so your players will know that the routine you've followed—and they're used to—works against every team, including the big ones.

Before we headed out of the dressing room, I thought of one more point to mention. It was a comment I would make only one other time in my coaching career, six years later, when we were to play Saint John's for the Catholic championship of Metropolitan Washington. Adrian Dantley was on that team, and he told his mother later that what I said fired him up so much he really wanted to take the floor and whip Saint John's.

"Fellas," I said, "everybody knows what DeMatha does in big games."

And then we took the floor.

The Greatest High School
Basketball Game Ever Played

Saint John DeMatha, pray for us.
Our Lady of Victory, pray for us.
—FROM THE DeMATHA PREGAME PRAYERS

Sometimes we take the floor before the other team, sometimes after, sometimes at the same time. It depends how I see the psychology of the situation. That night we took the floor first because I knew the crowd would be with us. I wasn't able to hear the reaction, however, because I never hurry out with my team. I lag behind on purpose, in order to say a silent prayer that I will be a good coach in this game, that I won't cheat the kids with a poor performance on my part, that I'll conduct myself like a gentleman and that God will be with me. An assistant coach takes charge of the warm-ups, and I walk onto the floor a few minutes later, usually after stopping at a water fountain for a drink, talking to a friend or two and generally in no hurry to reach the bench. When I got out there that night, I asked Frank Fuqua, then my assistant in charge of warm-ups, "What was the reaction?"

Frank's answer was the kind every coach likes to hear: "We have the crowd, and we'll have the game." That's the only way to go into the game, athlete or coach. Any other attitude and you're beaten before you start.

Again we stayed with our usual routine. As in every other game, we took the final minute before the opening whistle to say our usual prayers:

Remember, oh most gracious Virgin Mary, that never was it known that anyone who fled to your protection, implored your help, or sought your intercession, was left unaided. Inspired with this confidence, I fly to you, oh virgin of virgins, my mother. To you I come; before you I stand, sinful and sorrowful. Oh Mother of the Word Incarnate, despise not my petitions, but in your mercy, hear and answer me. Amen.

Hail Mary, full of grace, the Lord is with thee. Blessed are thou among women, and blessed is the fruit of thy womb, Jesus. Holy Mary, Mother of God, pray for us sinners, now and forever. Amen.

Saint John DeMatha, pray for us.
Our Lady of Victory, pray for us.

My starting five walked out to their positions, in front of that huge capacity crowd and the longest press table any of us had ever seen, not to mention the newspaper photographers and television camera crews lining each end of the court. We were only a few miles up the road along

Route 1 from DeMatha, but the real difference was immeasurable.

I looked at the first few rows behind me and found Kathy, my wife, only days away from the birth of our first child. It could have happened at any time, even that night, and I had an ambulance standing by just in case. We exchanged glances, then I looked around and up the aisles of that huge college field house and heard the ear-splitting noise as the referees moved to center court with the ball for the opening jump. Suddenly the thought struck me: "What's a kid from Silver Spring who used to coach at an orphanage doing in a spot like this?" But the thought was only fleeting. The game was about to start. It was time to go to work.

Both teams started slowly, feeling each other out, as you might expect from two teams in that kind of game. Both sides were playing superb defense, which made me confident, even though people were missing shots. We knew defense would win it for us if anything would. If our defense was working against Power, we knew we had a real chance. By the half, nothing had changed: still a low-scoring game, still close. We were ahead, 23–22. We walked across the floor toward the dressing room, and I looked back for Kathy. Still there.

As before the game, I let the players have their privacy in the dressing room at halftime. I never follow them into the dressing room. I let them go in alone and have a few moments to themselves to wind down and talk among themselves. While they're doing that, I get the halftime stats and look them over, then go to each assistant coach and ask his opinion on what went right, what went wrong and what we should concentrate on in the second half to win. I am emphatic about telling them that I want their honest advice, even if they think I made some mistakes out there myself. Being a coach doesn't mean you can't make mistakes. It only means that maybe you won't be aware of them, especially if you have made your staff of assistants afraid to tell you about them. I tell my assistants, "I want your opinion *now*. I don't want you telling me after the game what we should have done at the half. That doesn't help anybody. Tell me now, while it can still do some good."

Nobody really had anything to suggest at that halftime, though, because we had played an excellent half. Consequently, when I went into the locker room for the final few minutes before play started again, I simply told my team, "Fellas, you're doing a good, solid job. Our field goal percentage is not too good, but theirs isn't either, and that just reflects the excellent defense by both teams. Our job on the boards pleases me. There are no major areas of your performance I can criticize, but we have to do even *better* this half. We have to do an even *better* job of rebounding, and we have to do an even *better* job of running our players and we have to do an even *better* job of out-hustling Power at every turn—diving for loose balls, for instance. Basically, we're following the game plan perfectly. Just keep right on doing what you've been doing—only push yourselves to do even *better*.

"If that seems impossible, remember one thing: You've got a half to play, and a lifetime to remember it. Now let's go."

The second half was just as tight. With a minute and forty seconds to play, we were still leading, but by only two points, when Sid Catlett hit on a long jump shot and added a free throw to put us up by five, 41–36. A layup by Power closed it to 41–38, but Mickey Wiles sank two free throws and Sid tapped in a rebound and we were up by seven, 45–38, with less than a minute to go.

Suddenly, the speakers boomed, and the public address man came on with the same announcement as the year before—once again, he said, the crowd was watching the two most outstanding high school teams in America. And once again 12,500 people jumped to their feet with a deafening ovation.

And Kathy was still there.

With six seconds left, and our lead at five points, Power called a timeout. I walked to the scorer's table, my millionth trip there that night, it seemed, and said, "I just want to be sure. Is that their last time out?"

That was essential information. If it wasn't, the Panthers could throw a long pass and make a layup, cut our lead to three, then quickly call another timeout, still with four or five seconds left. It would still be possible for them to make a three-point play somehow on a steal and tie this thing after all. You can't *think* you know the situation in a spot like that. You have to *know* your information is correct.

The answer came back: Yes, that was Power's last timeout. I knew then we had the game won.

As I headed back down the court to our bench, I spotted Johnny Jones, a star on our 1961/62 team, who would later go on to two years with the champion Boston Celtics. He had come down out of the stands during the timeout and was talking to my team, standing in front of them as they sat on the bench. I wondered what the heck was going on. "Johnny," I said, "what are you doing?"

57

"Morgan," he said, "don't worry about a thing. I got it from here."

It broke me up, and while I was roaring with laughter, the greatest high school basketball game in history ended. The crowd sprang up, and I reached inside my coat for my victory cigar, just as I always do after a win. I hadn't known Auerbach all those years without learning something.

Avoiding the Letdown

Don't criticize success, analyze it.
—COLONEL RED BLAIK

That was one of Red Blaik's favorite sayings when, as head football coach at West Point, he was winning all those games, turning out stars like Glenn Davis and Doc Blanchard, and molding future head coaches like Vince Lombardi.

It's a favorite quote of Morgan Wootten's, too, and he promptly put it into practice after that Power game. He began to analyze his team's success so he could apply the formula in the future, a process that continued for years afterward, spurred on by the coaches—both high school and college—who called and wrote in to ask how he had done it, what had his preparation been, could they borrow the game films?

It was the only time since his freshman year that Lew Alcindor, the future Kareem Abdul-Jabbar, had been defeated. He would not be defeated again until three years later, January 20, 1968, in what is now called the greatest *college* basketball game ever played. That was when his UCLA Bruins under John Wooden had their forty-seven-game winning streak snapped by another present Washington area resident, Elvin Hayes, and the University of Houston.

The Wootten analysis of how DeMatha defeated Power Memorial on that January night in 1965 is clear and uncomplicated.

We did it by stopping Lew. It's that simple, and that's why I've never changed my strategy since. That convinced me: Stop the other team's big man by taking away its inside game and you have a good chance of winning. We fronted and backed Lew the entire game, sticking to our determination that if they were going to beat us, they'd have to find somebody else to do it. We cut off the Power passing lanes, we trapped, we did everything you could think of to deny him the ball, and it worked. We held him to sixteen points, and the last two of those only came because we gave him a layup in the final seconds so as not to foul him and give Power a three-point play. Lew had been averaging thirty points a game, which gives an idea of just how well our players had executed the game plan. Our final margin was three points, 46–43.

On defense, our success was due in large part to the good boxing out underneath the boards done by Sid Catlett and Bob Whitmore. Together they held Alcindor to fourteen rebounds, four fewer than the year before, while grabbing eighteen themselves.

A picture in the Washington *Star* the next day helped to tell the story of what happened. Our game was the top story in the sports section that Sunday morning, right below the big banner headline which read, DEMATHA

SNAPS POWER'S STREAK. Inside was a picture of Mickey Wiles lofting a shot over Lew's outstretched arm for a basket in the first quarter. John Moylan's tennis racket had paid off quickly.

After the game, we returned to DeMatha and had a party for the coaches and faculty of both schools. The Power people were just as gracious in defeat as they had been in victory, and all of us enjoyed what we knew had been a great experience for our kids and for ourselves, and we kept enjoying it until four in the morning. Jack Donohue, Power's coach, said he had seen trouble coming from the moment his group had arrived at Union Station in downtown Washington and we had met them with our cars to drive them to their hotel. I had prevailed upon two of my buddies, Rod Breedlove again and Walter Coughlin—a Secret Service agent in charge of Vice-President Hubert Humphrey's detail—to come along and add their cars to ours.

"Right then," Jack told the party, "I knew we were in trouble. The guy meets me at the train station with a star linebacker for the Washington Redskins and a Secret Service agent, and as if that's not enough, when we get to the gym in my rental car I notice that in the parking space for the visiting coach, there's an ambulance. I asked how come and somebody said, 'Oh, that's for Coach Wootten's wife in case she needs it.' How can you beat that combination?"

Donohue had some nice things to say about us in a serious vein, too. The next week *Newsweek* magazine had an article about the game with a picture of Lew being sandwiched between two Stags and standing empty-handed on offense. In the article, Jack praised our double-teaming defense against his big man, saying, "I don't think Lewie had the ball more than twelve or thirteen times all night (our game films show eleven). People are always trying that kind of defense against us, of course. But nobody has done it that well."

Jack, always a class guy, also made sure he had some nice things to say to Lew after the game. Alcindor was heartbroken and said, "It's all my fault," to which Donohue replied as a good coach, and a good human being, should: "You played the way you always have, Lewie. If you want the blame for this one, you'll have to take credit for the other seventy-one."

The quality of Bob Whitmore's defense against Lew came as no surprise. It was the kind of effort you knew would come from someone who worked as hard as Bob did, a boy willing to give up three hours a day just to get back and forth to school. He stayed confident that he could do the job, even after he saw Alcindor go "up and up and up" at that pregame meal. He knew he was prepared because he had paid the price beforehand in our practices. After our great victory, and his own, Bob said something significant. "I was playing a guy who was almost superhuman, but he didn't beat me. He knocked me down, but I kept getting up. That's what athletics teach you. You keep getting up." Bob ultimately received no fewer than one hundred and fifty scholarship offers and became the first black captain in the history of Notre Dame.

For the record, Kathy had our baby three days later—our first child, Cathy, followed since by four others, Carol, Patricia, Brendan and Joey. I'm sure she didn't mind postponing everything until after the Power game. By then she was used to that sort of thing. One day in 1964 not long before we were to be married she was in my office at DeMatha, leafing through the game book—the book every coach keeps, showing his schedule of practices, scrimmages and games—when she saw an entry for the day of the wedding:

May 16—at Blessed Sacrament. 10:00 A.M.

"Morgan," she said, laughing, "this makes it look as if our wedding was just another game."

"Oh, no, honey," I told her soberly, "that's a *big* game."

My starting five played that entire game, and I point to those five boys even today not just because of their tremendous athletic accomplishment that night, but because of their success in life afterward. They are an example of how participation in athletics can prime you for life. Every DeMatha team hears me tell of their successes—and they have been successful because they have always kept their priorities in order—God, family, school, basketball:

Bob Whitmore, center—Graduate of Notre Dame law
　　school, now a successful lawyer.
Sid Catlett, power forward—Notre Dame graduate,
　　now an executive with Motorola Corporation.
Bernie Williams, small forward—Graduate of LaSalle,
　　eight years in the ABA as a teammate of Julius
　　Erving, now an executive with Xerox Corpora-
　　tion.
Ernie Austin, guard—Graduate of Syracuse, now a
　　success in the restaurant business.
Mickey Wiles, guard—Graduate of the University of
　　Maryland, now a professional model and actor.

That team is now enshrined in the Basketball Hall of Fame in Springfield, Massachusetts, its picture installed there at the end of the season. Of course, there's no pleasing everyone. When I told John Moylan about the honor we were going to receive, he complained with a straight face, "My tennis racket should be in there, too."

After the Power triumph, the challenge became, as any coach would expect, how to avoid a letdown in the next game. Our opponent was Roosevelt High School, a Washington public school capable of knocking anybody off at any time. All of a sudden, they had the new top team in the nation in their sights, and they were licking their chops at the opportunity of upsetting us.

I had left the whole next week open on our schedule because I had expected us to need a week to recover, regardless of which way the Power game went. The M Club of the University of Maryland had put considerable pressure on me to reschedule the Power match so the club could use Cole Field House for a game between the Bullets and the Boston Celtics, but I had refused, because that would have undone a whole year's work for all of us. I had wanted that week before Power to get ready, and I wanted that week after Power to recover.

When I saw how flat we were for Roosevelt, however, even after a week off, I began to think maybe I had been wrong. Maybe I should have scheduled a game sooner; that way we might have snapped out of it. I don't know, and of course I'll never know.

Whatever the reason, the fact was that, at halftime of the Roosevelt game, we were losing and we were awful. In the last few seconds before we were to return to the floor, I tried to jolt our players out of it in the locker room. I said, "Look, fellas. We've had a lot of great moments together this season. It's been an unbelievable year. But if you want to pick this date to lose, and to this team, there's really not much I can do about it because it's your team."

That didn't reach them. They went out and sleepwalked their way through the third quarter. We were up by only one point against a team we really should have been defeating easily, and a one-point difference is never safe. All the ingredients were there for a stunning upset, one which would wash away all the achievement of only seven days before. People might say, "Well, maybe DeMatha was just lucky against Power. Maybe they're not really in the same class with Power if they can't be consistent." We had a whole lot riding on this Roosevelt game, and we were on the verge of blowing it.

For the first time in my career, I deliberately started riding the official, Bob Chick, to get him to call a technical foul on me. I questioned his every call, and with great emphasis. I never cussed, because I don't and I don't allow our players to. Any DeMatha player I hear saying anything wrong gets sent home immediately from practice and is not allowed to return until the following day. If it happens more than once, that guy is in the worst kind of trouble with me, and I don't care who he is. I tell our men, "There will be no cussing on this team. You're not going to hear it from me, and I don't want to hear it from you."

So I didn't cuss the ref, but I sure kept unloading on him. I think he knew what I had in mind, so he was slow to slap me with a technical, so slow that he only added to my frustration. Finally Bob had had enough and he blew his whistle, turned to me and said, "That's a technical, Morgan. I'm not going to let you talk to me like that."

While Roosevelt was shooting the technical, I got our team off to the side and said, "You want to know why the ref called the technical. Well, he called it because I got mad. And I got mad because I'm so embarrassed—for you. Everybody came here to see the team that beat Power. There are college scouts all through the stands. And you're making spectacles of yourselves. That's why I'm so embarrassed for you."

There wasn't any time for discussion because play was resuming, but as our players headed back onto the court, I heard Bob Whitmore say, "C'mon, men. A little class."

We won by fifteen.

My friend, partner and mentor, Joe Gallagher, doesn't completely agree with me about getting a technical foul called on yourself in order to fire up your team. Al McGuire, of course, made a whole career out of doing it, but in a book Joe has written called *High School Basketball: How to Be a Winner in Every Way*, he says, "I've never drawn a technical foul deliberately . . . I disagree with that tactic. I don't think there is ever a time when a technical foul helps your team."

Maybe so, but I can remember a few times when he didn't mind the technicals at all. One time, in a game against Saint John's, we stole the ball and drove downcourt for an uncontested layup. Joe jumped off the bench and screamed to the ref that his man had been fouled on the steal. The official slapped the T sign on him and then told the scorer the layup didn't count. I couldn't believe it, and I let the official, Bob Leamons, know about it. Then, to add to my temperature, we missed the free throw on Joe's technical. Then Saint John's stole an inbounds pass, drove the length of the court and scored. After the game, Joe was laughing as he said to me, "I figured that was a five-point play."

We won the game, but it was the hard way. I asked Leamons later, "Bob, why didn't you wait until after the layup? The play was still in motion and we were the ones with the ball, not Joe. Why take the layup away from the other team?"

He said, "You know, Morgan, I would have done that—if I had thought of it." Now you see why it's useless to argue with those guys.

On another occasion, we were playing Saint John's and losing because we kept getting called for lane violations on our free throws. We were getting the free throws because of a tactic I had invented in 1960 with John Herbert and later perfected with Mickey Wiles (who had used it in modified form against Lew Alcindor). It's called "taking the charge" and consists of the defender positioning himself in front of the man with the ball in such a way that the offensive man can't help but plow right into him, thus drawing an offensive foul for charging. It's since been copied at every level of basketball, from grade school to the pros, but it was invented right there on the basketball court at DeMatha.

It was new now, though, and Saint John's just couldn't handle it. They would run into us and we would make the free throws, but the officials kept blowing the whistle on us for stepping over the line before the shot. I've never seen so many lane violations called in one game in my life, more than you'd see in ten or twenty games put together.

Drastic measures were called for. In the fourth quarter, I took the four other players on the court and stuck them behind our foul-shooter any time we got a free throw, so their feet wouldn't go near the lane. It worked perfectly —we made sixteen out of sixteen. Rod Breedlove was at the game, and when he saw that he leaned over, tapped me on the shoulder and said, laughing, "Let's see Joe top that one."

With just a couple of minutes left, Joe was the one getting frustrated now. All game long his ball handlers had been running into DeMatha defenders, his men had been called for charging, and there I'd be, jumping off the bench to help the referee by yelling, "Charge!"

So he decided to get even. With time running out, we brought the ball inbounds after a Saint John's score. Mickey Wiles took the inbounds pass, turned and dribbled one time—and suddenly all five Saint John's players collapsed on the floor. At that precise moment, Joe leaped from his bench and screamed, "Charge!"

Breedlove tapped me on the shoulder, laughing even harder than before: "It's a tie."

That was definitely one-up for Joe—even though we won the game.

There's one more story I want to tell before getting back to more serious matters. One time in 1967 we were having a particularly tough time winning against a team I thought we should be beating. We were headed for a 28–1 season, but not that night. We weren't just losing, we were getting embarrassed: down by twenty-three points with seven minutes to go.

I called time out and told my players, "Look, fellas. We may win, we may lose. But can't we just play the best seven minutes of basketball possible? Even if we lose."

They responded with an incredible comeback, closing a twenty-three-point gap and even taking the lead, all within six minutes, so that by the time the final minute came, we were freezing our victory. After the game, I was talking to Frank Fuqua, my assistant, in the dressing room when something dawned on me. "My Lord, Frank, I said 'lose' to the players out there. I've never said that word in my life. I said 'lose.' Just think of what that could do to my coaching image and my career if that ever got out."

Nothing ever stumped Frank for very long. He leaned over and whispered to me, "Deny everything."

ABOVE: *Coach Morgan Wootten's first basketball team—the starting five for St. Joseph's Home for Boys. Wootten is at rear center.* PHOTO BY JACK EARLY.

RIGHT: *Bob Whitmore drives around Power Memorial's Lew Alcindor (33), now Kareem Abdul-Jabbar, in De Matha's 1965 victory in "the greatest high school basketball game ever played."* PHOTO BY HARRY NALTCHAYAN, WASHINGTON POST.

Adrian Dantley, later to become a star for Notre Dame, the U.S. Olympic team and the Los Angeles Lakers, scores high against Saint John's. PHOTO BY ART O'BRIEN.

The 1977-78 undefeated national championship team during its tour of Brazil, Rio de Janeiro in the background. PHOTO BY TERRY O'DRISCOLL.

The Woottens stand for inspection. From left are Joey, Brendan, Patricia, Carol and Cathy. Wife Kathy is at the sink. PHOTO BY TERRY ARTHUR. COURTESY PEOPLE WEEKLY © 1979 TIME INC.

Wootten with some of his students after a history class. PHOTO BY TONY TRIOLO. COURTESY SPORTS ILLUSTRATED © 1979 TIME INC.

...sing college options wtih Sidney Lowe and Brian Sheahan. PHOTO BY TRIOLO. COURTESY SPORTS ILLUSTRATED © 1979 TIME INC.

Reviewing game strategy at halftime, Jack Bruen at the door. PHOTO BY TONY TRIOLO. COURTESY SPORTS ILLUSTRATED © 1979 TIME INC.

The DeMatha pre-game huddle. PHOTO BY DELMA STUDIOS.

Coach Wootten emphasizes a point to center Percy White. PHOTO BY ROCCO ME

The 1978-79 DeMatha team, city champs for the fourteenth time in nineteen years. PHOTO BY TONY TRIOLO. COURTESY SPORTS ILLUSTRATED © 1979 TIME INC.

The Recruitment Rush:
Winning a College Scholarship

If you want to be a good parent, find out what your children want to do. If it's decent and honorable, advise them to do it.

—HARRY TRUMAN

Parents, coaches and athletes themselves all face a difficult time when successful ball players reach their senior year in high school and face the prospect of college recruitment. It can be a delightful experience, one which sets the athlete firmly on the road to a lifetime of success and financial security—or it can be sheer torture, a nightmare which may spell disaster for his entire career.

College recruiters play for keeps, and in this tough league, Morgan Wootten's record is unmatched, even undreamed of. For the past nineteen years, every senior on his basketball team, including every substitute, has won a full four-year college scholarship, and this includes schools such as Duke, North Carolina, Notre Dame, Georgia Tech, Maryland, Harvard, North Carolina State, Georgetown, American University, Catholic University, Clemson, Kansas, Princeton, William and

Mary, Virginia, Pitt, Temple and LaSalle, to name just a few.

How does Morgan Wootten do it—and how does he protect the player during his senior year so that the recruiters don't hound the man to death, ruin his last year of high school, even jeopardize the young man's performance as an athlete? For the high school coach who finds himself with his first blue-chip athlete, the parents who have never been through anything like this before, and the athlete who is suddenly the center of attention, Wootten has some advice on how to handle things—and how not to.

I'd had almost no experience in this recruiting business until Johnny Herbert came along in my fourth year at De-Matha. Ernie Cage had been recruited in my second season there, and won a full scholarship to Mount Saint Mary's in the Maryland mountains, but he was the only player in those first few seasons the recruiters had been after. Johnny Herbert was becoming a very hot prospect, though, so I thought I'd better be organized and prepared for the feelers that were bound to come to him and to some of his teammates on our 1960/61 team.

When that season started, I wrote a mimeographed letter, with a paragraph in it about each senior on the team, and mailed it to more than three hundred colleges. I told the coaches at those schools that our practices were open and enclosed a copy of our schedule. It worked. The scouts started showing up from time to time, and one of those times happened to be on a night when John scored thirty-seven points against Bladensburg, a public school in our county. The result was a full scholarship to Georgia Tech. From then on, the floodgates were open. John is a successful builder and businessman in the Atlanta area today, and a street in one of his subdivisions is named Morgan Street.

I would definitely recommend this approach to any beginning coach, or one with his first blue-chipper, and advise that he get the letter in the mail early in September. Be totally candid in describing each player's pluses and minuses, and in adding your opinion about what level of ball the boy is qualified to play. The end of the season is too late for this. The student can't legally try out, and since you probably didn't film your games, the college scout will have nothing to see for himself and your senior will be out of luck. The scouts must be able to see your senior perform. Julius Erving had only two college offers, from Columbia and Massachusetts, because he was tucked away at a little-known high school and the recruiters had simply never heard of him. The letter technique overcomes this risk, but they must go out just after Labor Day. After you have established yourselves as a winning team over several seasons, you won't have to send out letters any more. The scouts will start coming to you.

Coaches have a three-fold responsibility to their outstanding seniors: to work hard to get them the best scholarship offers possible, to give them the best guidance possible in making their decision and to protect them from the inevitable pressures which recruiting will cause.

To protect the kids from those pressures—and they can become unbelievable if you don't control the situation as coach—I sit down with all of my seniors before the season starts and set out these basic rules:

1. Do not give out your address, phone number or academic record to anyone. That's confidential information and you have every right in the world to keep it that way.

2. If a scout wants to talk to a player, the scout has to go through me. He won't get any confidential information from me, but I'll let him talk to the boy for five or ten minutes after practice in the gym. Period. If a scout calls on the phone, I tell him I'll relay the message to the player, and if the player wants to talk to the scout, he'll return the call, collect, and at his convenience—not the scout's. Any wining and dining is illegal now under the rules of the National Collegiate Athletic Association, and anything else is illegal under *my* rules.

3. Seniors must complete a questionnaire which tells me what they want in a college. In it should be their academic, athletic and social requirements, any restrictions they might have as to the distance of the college, and any other special considerations they might have in mind.

With this information, I can save everybody a lot of wasted time, including the scouts. If a West Coast school asks about a kid who has said he wants to stay in the East in his questionnaire, I tell the scout. I've done him a favor and the boy, too.

Before the season begins I sit down with the parents, as well, to go over these rules and to suggest that they put the responsibility of communicating with the army of scouts in my hands. Otherwise, they'd find them descending on their sons and themselves at all hours of the day and night seven days a week until the end of the school year nine months away. That's a long time to hold up under that strain, and the truth is that they often don't hold up.

Using the information from the questionnaire, then, and my own knowledge of the boy's personality and ability, we—the boy, his parents and myself—weed the offers down to a manageable list of ten or so. That can be a pretty tough

79

job in itself because in some cases athletes get as many as three hundred college offers. Once we've trimmed the list, the boy can start deciding what campuses he wants to visit. NCAA rules limit him to six. I let our seniors make one or two campus visits in the fall if they want to, but after November 8 no more until the end of the season. They don't need that kind of distraction while they are playing their schedule.

I also have a rule about those visits: Don't make your decision while you're on a campus. A seventeen-year-old high school kid can get pretty excited walking around a college campus and seeing the beautiful layout, the fancy gym, the fraternity houses and the good-looking girls, while he dreams of becoming the Big Man on Campus. That's no environment in which to make a calm and rational decision. My message to the athlete is to enjoy the trip, see and learn all he can, talk to other players already there—including second- and third-stringers—and to students who are not athletes, learn as much as he can about the curriculum and the school's academic reputation, see whether it offers the courses he thinks he'll want to take, talk to the professors, do everything he can to find out everything possible about that school. Then thank the coach and come home. That's where the boy'll be able to make his best decisions.

Adrian Dantley's experience is a case in point. He was deluged with offers but had just about settled on North Carolina as his choice. The NCAA rules allowed him one more visit, and he had promised the Notre Dame officials he'd go out there and talk to them, but after visiting UNC and Dean Smith, Adrian wasn't sure a trip to Notre Dame would be worth the trouble. "You know, Morgan," he told me, "I really like North Carolina, and I'm pretty sure I want to go to school there."

I said, "You didn't agree to anything while you were there, did you?" Adrian said, "No, I remembered the rule about that. I told Coach Smith I would call him and let him know my decision, but that I liked what I saw tremendously and that I might wind up picking North Carolina as my college."

I reminded him, though, that he had promised Digger Phelps and the rest of Digger's Notre Dame staff that he'd go out there. I thought he should keep his promise, have a good time, then come back to DeMatha and make up his mind.

So he went. The next thing I knew he was calling me from South Bend to say, "Morgan, I love this place. This is where I want to go. There's no doubt about it."

Again I asked if he had agreed to anything. Again he said no. He came back home and, together with his mother, Virginia, his aunt and me, he was able to assess his situation and his offers calmly—and he picked Notre Dame.

Another recruiting rule of mine is simple: The boy makes the decision for himself. The parents don't decide, and neither does the coach. One of the worst mistakes any parent can make is to *tell* the boy where he's going to college. If things don't work out, he'll never forgive his parents for forcing him to go to that school. They can offer advice and suggestions, but it must be his decision. That advice from Harry Truman at the top of this chapter is right on the mark: "If you want to be a good parent, find out what your children want to do. If it's decent and honorable, advise them to do it."

With only a few exceptions, the scouts are good and honorable people. In almost every case they'll honor your rules and respect you for doing it your way because they know it's best for the student, and it gives every scout an equal chance. I bend over backward to be fair with them. Even if I have a blue-chipper who will obviously be going to a big-time college, I take time to talk to the smaller schools. No scout from a small school gets a brushoff. If you make that mistake, and the next year you're looking for a good small-school offer for one of your boys, those scouts will simply tell you they'll see you later. Instead, I tell the scout from a small school, "John has filled out our questionnaire for seniors and he wants to go to a big school, but if you want to talk to him for a few minutes, I'll be happy to make the arrangements." That approach and courtesy might help get you what you want next year.

It used to be that colleges would send their scouts to your school on a special plane. Sometimes it wasn't even a scout, but the head coach himself. You and your prospect would be wined and dined, and you, as the coach, would find yourself putting on some weight from all that good eating. That's all forbidden now, and I'm in favor of that—but I sure miss all those good meals.

On rare occasions when I do find a scout or coach breaking either the NCAA rules or mine, I bar him from De-Matha—permanently. I tell all comers, "Don't thank us if you get the athletes—and don't blame us if you don't. We don't *send* anybody anywhere. We don't tell them whom to marry or where to go to school."

I remember one confrontation when a scout came to visit me in my office at DeMatha and said point blank, "I figure your two (Bob Whitmore and Bernard Williams, on the 1964/65 team which beat Power) could be worth five thousand dollars." I threw him right out of my office. Then I called his coach—it was a Midwestern school—and confronted him: "Your man was in here and put his money right on the table. It's your responsibility as coach to prevent that. Our players are not for sale. Your school is finished at DeMatha."

Another time, that same season, a coach from an Eastern college came to our gym, also interested in Whitmore and Williams. I told him Whitmore was home sick, but he could talk to Williams in the gym for a few minutes. After that, with my approval, he took Bernard to dinner, in the days when you could still do that.

The next day, both players were home sick, not just Whitmore. The coach had gone to Bob's home and talked him into going out to dinner, too, with Bernard and him. The result was that Bernard had caught Bob's bug. That coach did it without asking or telling me, knowing all the time that we were still playing our schedule and that we had an undefeated season going. He also knew full well that we were scheduled to play the freshman team from American University of Washington that day—and now my two stars were home sick.

I felt obligated to tell American what had happened, so I called them to say we'd be there that afternoon as scheduled, but we'd be minus our two big attractions. They said they'd rather play us when we were at full strength, so we rescheduled the game and made it next to last on our schedule. When it finally rolled around, we did beat them, but as a result of the rescheduling, our last game was the very next day, and it was also against a college team, the Maryland freshmen. Asking a high school team to defeat two college freshman teams in two days after playing its entire schedule is just asking too much. We lost to Maryland in our last game—by one point. There went our undefeated season.

That's not the end of the story about that coach, however. Two weeks later, he became coach at a Big Ten school and had the nerve to ask if there was still a chance to get Whitmore and Williams. I was relieved to be able to tell him, "No, I'm sorry. We have a press conference scheduled for tomorrow to announce that Bob is going to Notre Dame and Bernard to LaSalle." He thanked me and that was that—I thought.

When the boys showed up at school the next day, Bob complained that he was tired. I asked him why and he said, "Coach X called me up and kept me on the phone until after midnight." That coach has since been promoted to athletic director at his school, but that's one Big Ten university which won't get a DeMatha player as long as that guy is there. And if he moved to another school again, then *that* college won't get a DeMatha player. I don't tell any of my seniors where to go to college, but I sure tell them where *not* to go. I won't let them make the mistake of going to a school that has a coach or a scout like that. I don't want my kids playing for dishonest people who break rules or go behind your back.

My players always feel the same way I do and make their selections accordingly, especially after I tell them, "People like that are breaking the rules to try to get you. And as soon as somebody else comes along, somebody who's a little better than you are or a little taller, or you get hurt, who knows what they'll do with you? They may dump you from the team and take your scholarship away from you. Then where would you be? And as for any offers of cash, remember this: If they buy you, they might sell you."

A dramatic illustration of what can happen if you don't protect the privacy of your seniors and their families—the most extreme case I ever experienced—involved James Brown, our blue-chip star of the late 1960s, whose success inspired a neighborhood kid down the street to come to DeMatha a few years later when he reached the ninth grade—Adrian Dantley.

James was in a summer camp before his senior year at DeMatha and somehow his phone number got out and the coaches and scouts picked it up through their grapevine. He was a great college prospect, and as a result overrecruited all year long. The pressure on him was even greater than those around him realized, however, including me. This became evident near the end of the season, when we were playing in the semifinals of the Knights of Columbus tournament in Washington. Early in the game, James took himself out and complained that he was tired. I was surprised that he could tire so early in the game when I knew he was in excellent condition, a requirement which I demand of all my players. He went to the bench and sat down as the game resumed. The next thing I knew, I heard some commotion and I looked down the bench to see James collapsed on the floor.

He was carried out on a stretcher and taken to Providence Hospital by ambulance. The cause? Exhaustion. He had been up too late on too many nights with too many scouts. They simply would not leave him alone, and that's exactly what happens if you let the player's name or address become known.

We won that game, with our star flat on his back in a hospital bed, but the next night we were scheduled to play McKinley Tech of Washington for the tournament championship. Tech had whipped us soundly by fifteen points earlier in the year, with James in our lineup. Without him, the prospects were dreary indeed. Some of my friends called to apologize and said they weren't coming to that game, but they were sure I would understand. They said they couldn't cope with the thought of seeing De-Matha blown out.

That Sunday we played one of the greatest games any DeMatha team has *ever* played. Our players left James' chair on the bench empty, with his warm-up jacket draped over it, and Mark Edwards moved into James' spot in the lineup. He was six feet four inches tall, but he spent the game outrebounding two opponents who were both six eight. At the half, we were leading by twenty-one points.

I was getting a drink at a water fountain during half-time while my players rested in their dressing room, when I heard a fan behind me saying in a loud voice—obviously for my benefit—"The way I figure it, if we can cut De-Matha's lead to ten by the end of the third quarter, Tech can still win." I turned around, because he seemed so anxious to get a response from me, and said, "I've got news for you. This game is already history." I don't like to be cocky, but I don't like to be insulted, either.

We won that tournament in a romp, and as the tournament officials were presenting the championship trophies to our players, James Brown came down and accepted his

86

in person. He had sneaked out of the hospital and watched the whole game from up in the stands, unknown to any of us.

As it turns out, James' final choice of college furnishes yet another illustration of my rule about not making a decision while you're still on a particular college's campus. He visited North Carolina and, like Adrian Dantley, liked everything about it, including the Tar Heels' coach, Dean Smith, a man rich in class and integrity. James remembered the rule, however, and told Dean, "Coach, I'm 99 percent sure I'll come here, but I'll call you after I get back to let you know for sure."

Sure enough, after he got back home, Senator Ted Kennedy called me at DeMatha and invited James and me to visit him in his office in the Senate. We went down to Capitol Hill and had an enjoyable visit and Senator Kennedy talked James into visiting Harvard University, the Senator's alma mater. James did, and that's where he went to college. He had avoided the mistake of committing himself to one school too soon.

Dean Smith missed out on him, but he keeps trying—always open and aboveboard with the player and his family and me, the kind of coach you'd want your own son to play for in college because of his great example and good influence on his players.

Lefty Driesell is another one. Lefty, like Dean, kept trying for years to come up with a DeMatha player and kept missing. They both tried hard for Adrian Dantley and were in the running right up to the end, but both lost out. No alibis from them, no hard feelings. They always came back the next year and tried again, and in Lefty's case, he finally scored with Dutch Morley, the point guard on our undefeated national championship team of 1977/78. Lefty always places a lot of emphasis on making sure his players "have their heads on straight," as he puts it. He talks to them about total effort, but also about accepting the will of God whatever happens. He has them write a composition for him at the beginning of their freshman year on what they want to achieve at the University of Maryland—whether in basketball or in another area—just because he is convinced you have to have a goal if you are to be a success. Dean Smith and Lefty Driesell and coaches like them are always welcome at DeMatha because, to use Lefty's words, they have their heads on straight.

For parents, the problems of recruiting are somewhat different, but just as important. It's something that has never happened to them before. It's pretty heady stuff to have a big-name college coach or a bank president or a congressman or even Senator Kennedy call them up or come to their home. If their boy is playing under an experienced coach who has gone through this recruiting business enough times before, and is the kind of coach who shares their sense of values, then they have no problem. In that case, my advice is: Let the coach handle things, in coordination with you. Follow his advice. If you try to cope with this unbelievable strain yourself, the player will become distracted and worn out, he'll hurt himself in his school work and his athletic performance, he'll hurt his team and he may ruin his college prospects with a bad year. If your coach is successful, intelligent and experienced, and you respect him for all the important reasons, you are far better off letting him carry the burden, then discussing your choices with him after the season and the campus visits, and then letting the boy himself decide where he wants to go to college.

But what if you don't have an experienced coach? What if your coach has never worked with college recruiters before? What if he's the kind who cuts off all scouts until the season is over, which means it's unlikely they'll ever get a chance to see your son in action? In that case, the parents must step in and talk to the coach, then decide how to proceed; perhaps the parents will have to become the buffer themselves instead of the coach. In any case, the home address and phone number should still be kept confidential or else the athlete may well find himself in the same predicament James Brown did.

Another danger to look out for, and it happens more than most people realize, is the package deal: The coach tells a college scout or coach, "If you want my player, you'll have to take me, too." Those guys want a job at that college as an assistant basketball coach or some other position, and they're willing to use an innocent high school kid and his family to get it. That's bad news. There should be a rule against it, and it's hard to believe that there isn't. It's not your responsibility, or your son's, to get a better job for your high school coach. And what'll happen to your boy a year or two later when the assistant leaves or the head coach is fired and all the assistants replaced? If your boy's high school coach can't get a job on his own, you shouldn't do it for him.

A good coach who is aware of his moral responsibilities to his seniors will spend a lot of his time each year working in their behalf. He'll get all those calls and visits and correspondence, then he'll sit down with the players and their families and work his way through the offers with them and weigh each one. In those seasons when I have a good crop of seniors, I may spend up to 30 percent of my total basketball time on recruiting matters. But it's worth it, not only because of what you owe that player and his family, but—from the practical standpoint—because if you don't act as the buffer for your seniors, you're going to hurt not only them but your whole team.

I've already told how Adrian Dantley decided to go to Notre Dame, but his full story is worth telling here because it illustrates the entire range of problems and opportunities and questions involved in the recruiting of an outstanding—in fact, in the true sense of the word, great—high school sports star.

Many fans don't realize it, but high school stars are as famous in their own way as college and professional players. They are selected for All-American teams, just like the college players; scouted by the colleges, just as the college players are scouted by the pros; and receive offers, just as on the other levels. The people interested in them have as many scouting reports and details on them as any pro team has on their prospects.

In the case of Adrian Dantley, he was well known to the college scouts as early as the ninth grade, when he was only fourteen years old. Because he lived down the street from James Brown, he had decided he wanted to go to DeMatha, just likes James. It's a chain reaction that happens all the time. Right now they're saying, "I want to go to DeMatha and be the next Adrian Dantley."

I was watching a summer-league game in 1969 when Paul Furlong, the basketball coach at Mackin High School, one of the teams in our Catholic Metro Conference, walked over to me and said, "You're the luckiest guy in the world." I asked him the obvious question, because I didn't have the slightest idea what he was talking about. He said, "There's a boy in summer school at DeMatha who will be the greatest player you've ever coached." I asked his name. "Adrian Dantley," he said. I'd never heard of him. (This should put to rest, incidentally, the old story that we recruit players; if I did, I certainly would have known about Dantley. We have never recruited, nor offered scholarships—both are against conference rules—nor have rich alumni ever "sponsored" a boy's tuition.)

When I inquired more about this Dantley boy, I found out about his idolization of James Brown. He had a long way to go to be the next James Brown, though. He was chunky fat and on the slow side—but the potential was there, especially the great hands and fierce desire. I knew that after watching him for only ten minutes in our first practice.

Another one to spot his potential immediately was Jim Phelan, the coach at Mount Saint Mary's. Jim saw Adrian play against Good Counsel, another school in our league, in one of our first games. Adrian had not only made our team as a ninth grader, he had made it as a starter—a fourteen-year-old among some of the best high school basketball players in America. After that Good Counsel game, Phelan got my okay to talk to this kid.

After introducing himself, he said, "Adrian, I want you to know that even though you're only a ninth grader, you have a full scholarship to Mount Saint Mary's four years from now." Adrian didn't know it at the time, but it was the same offer Jim had made a few years earlier to Rick Barry. Jim had coached Barry's older brother and kept him on his scholarship even after the boy had hurt himself and been forced to quit basketball. The Barry parents remembered that, and when Rick started playing high school ball in New Jersey, their only hope was that he would be good enough to play at Mount Saint Mary's. He wasn't even a starter until his senior year in high school, but once he cracked the starting lineup, there was no stopping him. He hit for something like eighteen points in his first game as a starter, then twenty-eight—and on he went. People stopped talking about Mount Saint Mary's. He went to Miami University, then on to NBA stardom with the Golden State Warriors and Houston Rockets.

Jim knew full well he wouldn't get Dantley either, but he wanted to get there first, for what it was worth, and offered a college scholarship to a fourteen-year-old boy. He told Adrian, "I just want you to remember who offered you your first scholarship." That made Jim Phelan the first coach to spot greatness in both Rick Barry and Adrian Dantley—and he missed out on both of them.

As a sophomore and again as a junior, Adrian kept getting better and better faster and faster. His determination and desire were without limit. He knew what he wanted and what he had to do to get there, and he was willing to pay the price. He practiced on his own, ran on his own, did calisthenics on his own, lifted weights on his own, jumped rope and ran up and down stadium steps on his own. One Christmas afternoon he came by my house and got the key to DeMatha's gym so he could squeeze in a workout by himself. He had developed a nose for the ball, and he had that desire which could change a weakness into a strength. And the best part of it all: He was a good person, and a good student.

That drive to excel stood out in the classroom as well as on the basketball court. Once, in my world history class, he knocked the daylights out of a test and scored ninety-eight, when the next highest score was only eighty. Another time he scored so well I was suspicious, so I started grilling him with other questions. He fired all the right answers back, but grew more resentful with each question, and after I quit he said, "You thought I cheated, didn't you?" You could see the anger in his tight jaw and his flashing eyes.

To be honest, I really did have to wonder because his performance on that test had been so superior—I had made that test as hard as I could to see how the class would respond. Adrian had simply gone home and studied history for three hours.

That performance revealed two things about Adrian Dantley: his determination to achieve his goals and his equal determination to gain a good education for himself. After leaving Notre Dame as a hardship case following his junior year, this same determination prompted him to return to Notre Dame after his rookie year in the NBA and earn his degree.

After those experiences in the classroom with him, I knew that here was a very special person, one who would win a championship in whatever he went into because there simply would be no stopping this guy.

Before Adrian's senior year, I told him and his family that if he thought those past two seasons had been something, he hadn't seen anything yet. All those letters he had already received from colleges would be just so much scrapbook material compared to the offers he was going to get as a senior, especially if he continued to work hard and take good care of himself. I really didn't have to add that last part because I knew he would.

Adrian had a superb senior year and so did we, and the letters were almost like snowflakes, so many of them came floating down on Adrian. The mail didn't swamp him, however, because it all came to me at DeMatha, not to his home, and I passed it on to him at a time and pace which I could control. We'd talk about each of them in a calm and relaxed atmosphere, and weed out many right off the bat because they didn't meet the preferences Adrian had spelled out in his questionnaire.

He finally narrowed his list down to the six campus visits he wanted to make: Minnesota, Southern California, North Carolina, North Carolina State, Notre Dame and Maryland. He almost decided at first to go to Maryland. His original preference had been to go away to school, which would have eliminated Maryland, only ten or fifteen minutes up Route 1 from his home, but Lefty Driesell, who has no equal as a recruiter, kept pouring on his charm and Adrian wavered. Finally, Adrian said he had made a firm decision. Despite the attractive picture which Lefty had painted, and Adrian's (and his mother's) fondness for Lefty himself, he had decided to go away after all. He asked me to tell Lefty that Maryland was now out of the running. I told him I'd call.

The next night, Adrian called me at my home, speaking in a hushed tone. "Morgan, have you told Lefty yet that I've eliminated Maryland?"

I told him no, that I had Driesell on my list of calls to make the next day.

Adrian said, "Well, don't call him yet."

I asked why.

"Because he's over here with a Maryland uniform with my name and number on it, and a warm-up jacket with my name on that, too."

That's pretty dazzling in the eyes of a high school kid. Lefty was pulling out all the stops. That uniform gimmick was a new one on me, and it darn near worked, as shown by the fact that Adrian had sneaked out of the room to the telephone to tell me to hold everything. Eventually, however, he stuck to his determination to go away to school. That's the only reason Adrian Dantley never played on the same Maryland team as John Lucas, Len Elmore and Tom McMillan.

Having decided to go to an out-of-town school, Adrian began to look seriously at North Carolina, but the Tar Heels were not at the top of his list immediately. Dean Smith had talked to Adrian at one point about playing both ends of the court—doing as much on defense as on offense, and vice versa. It's an aspect of the game that Dean, being the thorough coach that he is, and a champion, as a result, emphasizes, and he hadn't meant to imply any criticism of Dantley. He had just wanted Adrian to know what would be expected of him at North Carolina; but that's not the way Adrian took it. He had me call Dean Smith and tell him he had scratched North Carolina from his list.

Until the final decision is reached and the announcement made, however, you never really know for sure about the student's choice. In this case, Adrian called me about a week later and asked me to phone Dean again and tell him North Carolina was back in the running. He had re-evaluated things, and the Tar Heels were still alive and in first place.

I called Dean to give him the good news, but this time

he had a surprise for me. I said, "I have some really good news for you. You're back in the running with Adrian Dantley, and I think you're on top in his thinking."

Dean said, "Oh, no."

"What do you mean, 'Oh, no'? What's the matter? Don't you have any scholarships left?"

"No, it's not that," Dean said. "I just signed a kid yesterday who had one last question before we reached agreement: 'Is Adrian Dantley coming here to school? Because if he is, I'm not.' I told him no, that Adrian had turned us down."

Then Coach Smith told me, "There's no way in the world I could bring myself to get back into the running for Adrian after telling that kid what I did."

A lot of other coaches would have said to themselves, "I'll get Dantley now and worry about what I told the other kid later. This way I've got two hot prospects."

Not all of us—coaches or people in other professions with a similar chance—would have had the class and integrity to be totally frank with the kid and then equally frank with me. What he was telling me was that, to keep its good faith, North Carolina was *withdrawing* from the recruiting of Adrian Dantley, even though he knew his school probably could get him. All Dean had to say was yes, and he would have gotten the player called the most outstanding high school basketball star in the United States that year. He passed all that up, however, because of something he had told a kid the day before.

As things turned out, other factors ruled Adrian's decision anyway and, as I described earlier, he picked Notre Dame.

Shortly after he got back from the campus, we held a

huge press conference in DeMatha's library and announced the decision. Adrian said the top attraction, as far as he was concerned, was Notre Dame's outstanding academic program. The second reason, as you can imagine, was the excellence of its basketball program, and the tough national schedule the Irish play, promising Adrian the television, newspaper and magazine coverage which he would need if he was to become a star in the pros. That was always his other top goal—to become a star in the NBA—and he was certain that Notre Dame would provide the means to reach it.

He has reached it. He became a star in his first year in the pros, after a standout college career. None of this surprises anyone who really knows him, yet there was always a surprising number of people at each step of Adrian's development who said he'd never make it to his next goal. When he was a pudgy ninth grader at DeMatha, they said he'd never succeed, so he made high school All-American and All-Metropolitan, and became the best high school player in America. Then they said he would never succeed in college—too heavy, too slow, not quick enough, can't shoot from the outside, only six feet five inches tall—so he made the freshman All-American team and stayed All-American as a sophomore and a junior. How many players can you name who were college All-Americans in their sophomore years? Wilt Chamberlain, Jerry Lucas, Oscar Robertson, Kareem Abdul-Jabbar, Pete Maravich, Elvin Hayes—and Adrian Dantley. Pretty good company.

Then he confounded the skeptics once again by leading the United States team to the gold medal in the 1976 Olympics, along with his DeMatha teammate, Kenny Carr, who had become a star in his own right at North Carolina State.

97

It is the only time in the history of the Olympics that two stars from the same high school team made the United States squad. Adrian was the United States team's leading scorer.

How did Adrian accomplish so much? He tells it best in his own words. After the Olympics, Adrian came home to Washington and paid a visit to the Metropolitan Basketball Camp which Joe Gallagher and I conduct in several sessions each summer at Saint John's. I asked Adrian to bring his gold medal along to show the kids what hard work can do, and then he told them the story of how he had made the Olympic team.

He had reported to the team for tryouts, he said, thinking he had already paid the price with his hard work at DeMatha and Notre Dame. He found out that wasn't enough, however.

"I thought I was in great shape, but Dean Smith wanted more than great shape. He wanted more than a lot of great players really understood. A lot of them didn't make the Olympic squad because they didn't get the message.

"Dean Smith and the Olympic committee didn't pick the twelve best players for the United States team. He took the twelve best players who would play together. I never worked harder at anything in my life. I understood what the man said when I got to the tryout camp in North Carolina. I'd worked hard all my life and I wasn't about to stop now. I'd listened all my life. I had been coachable.

"I've always been coachable. When Dean Smith said he didn't want everyone throwing the ball up, shooting, he meant he didn't want shooting. For the first five scrimmages, Adrian Dantley didn't shoot. Guess that fooled all those guys who were waiting for Dantley to put 'em up. I didn't even look at the basket. I passed. I set screens. I cut in and out. I never had so many assists in my life.

"Some other guys didn't do what the coaches said. They kept shooting. Rickey Green of Michigan was one. Man, can that guy put them up. He scored thirty-four one night, thirty-five the next. The pro scouts were drooling. But you know what? Green was cut. He took twenty-eight shots one night and Dean Smith warned everyone that he wasn't looking for all that shooting. Not on a team of All-Stars. Green didn't sacrifice. You got to do what the coaches say."

That's Adrian Dantley to a tee. Do what the coaches say and work hard. That's why he's where he is today, an NBA star with the Los Angeles Lakers after being voted Rookie of the Year, despite the predictions, again, that he wouldn't make it in the pros.

Adrian wasn't my only outstanding senior in 1973, however. I had a bumper crop that year and I spent a big chunk of my time making sure I did right by them. We kept our streak going by getting full scholarships for all seven of them:

Bill Langloh—A starter all four of his years at Virginia.

Ron Satterthwaite—Twice voted Player of the Year in the Southern Conference while starring at William and Mary.

Kenny Roy—A football star at Maryland after receiving college scholarship offers in both football and basketball.

Buzzy O'Connell—One of the top three foul-shooters

in the nation for two seasons as he led Stetson to
the best record of any major independent college in the country.

Carroll Holmes—A star at Northern Illinois whose
rebounding at DeMatha made him known as
"Chairman of the Board."

Larry Nader—An outstanding guard all four of his
years at Penbrook State.

There was a junior on that team as well, named Kenny
Carr, with the same drive as Adrian Dantley. He had
banged up his knee as a sophomore, and Dr. Stan Lavine,
who is not only our team physician but the same for the
University of Maryland, the Washington Redskins and
the Washington Bullets, had said he didn't think Kenny
would ever be able to play basketball again. Kenny had
worked hard all summer at our camp, but still wasn't back
far enough along to start for us at the beginning of that
season. He kept at it, however, until his comeback was
complete, won a starting spot before midseason, and kept
right on going through his senior year and then on to NC
State.

I'm as proud of *all* these boys as their own parents are,
and one of the things that pleases me most, as much as
their basketball success, is that they are good, wholesome
people. They've always been courteous and respectful to
others, and they've conducted themselves in an exemplary
way, a way that reflects great credit on their families, their
schools and, most of all, themselves.

That's important, because if you can't acquire success
while remaining a good person, then you haven't really
been successful, and your scoring average or the amount

of money you're making doesn't change it. You've failed in life even if you've succeeded on the basketball court, and you're going to be living a lot longer than you're going to be playing basketball.

It's one of the themes I stress the most at DeMatha, both to my players and to my history students, and there's a poem I give out to my athletes which emphasizes it as well:

TO ANY ATHLETE

There are little eyes upon you
And they're watching night and day.
There are little ears that quickly
Take in every word you say;
There are little hands all eager
To do anything you do;
And a little boy who's dreaming
Of the day he'll be like you.

You're the little fellow's idol;
You're the wisest of the wise.
In his little mind about you,
No suspicions ever rise.
He believes in you devoutly,
Holds that all you say and do
He will say and do, in your way
When he's a grownup like you.

There's a wide-eyed little fellow,
Who believes you're always right,
And his ears are always open,
And he watches day and night.

You are setting an example
Every day in all you do,
For the little boy who's waiting
To grow up to be like you.

Corny? I don't think so. Neither does Adrian Dantley. When he went to Notre Dame, he took a copy of the poem with him.

How to Build a Winner

Success is failure turned inside out . . .
—FROM A POEM GIVEN TO DeMATHA PLAYERS

One look at the DeMatha record, even a brief glance, is enough to tell you why the Stags and Morgan Wootten enjoy the stature they do. It's hard to come up with an adequate adjective to describe a basketball record like this:

- 626 wins
- Four national high school championships
- Sixty championships in twenty-three seasons
- Ranked in the top ten Catholic high schools for sixteen straight years
- National Catholic champions five times
- Number one in Metropolitan Washington, including both public and private schools, thirteen of the past eighteen years

The New York Yankees, the Green Bay Packers of Vince Lombardi, the Boston Celtics, the UCLA Bruins of John Wooden—all domineering champions—had lapses, dry spells, even if brief, when they did not dominate as expected and someone else was able to claim the championship trophy. But DeMatha has not. Year after year they are the team to beat, locally and nationally, and the result is a record probably unequaled by any other athletic team in any sport.

This is how Wootten made it happen. First . . .

---

1. You have to have good people, people who will bring not just ability to their jobs but integrity, dedication to hard work and a good team attitude toward the whole operation and everyone in it. Any successful program in any field starts with that requirement. If you don't have good people, you won't make it. You may get lucky from time to time, or even over a stretch, but it won't last.

In high school, and even in college, that means starting with the good student-athletes, those who excel in the classroom as well as on the basketball court, who possess a fierce sense of competition coupled with a real desire to seek a good education.

DeMatha has several advantages now because of its winning record and its academic reputation. Classes are small and the atmosphere is that of a small school, even though we have the facilities of a big school. We receive more applications than any other independent high school in the Washington region because we are so strong in both areas.

2. The second major requirement is to attract superior assistant coaches, not just good ones but outstanding ones. We have had many over the years, men who have contributed as much to DeMatha's success and development as any of the rest of us. We know it because of our record, because of the continued success of our student-athletes after they graduate from DeMatha and because of the achievements of the coaches themselves in their later careers. Eddie Fogler, Dean Smith's assistant at North Carolina; Frank Fuqua, formerly at Georgetown; Terry Truax at Colorado; Marty Fletcher, the top assistant at NC State; Bill Mecca at Quinnipiac College; Murray Arnold, head coach at U. of Chattanooga; Perry Clark, assistant at Penn State; Ray Hite, at Western Kentucky; and his brother, Bill Hite, at VPI—they all worked or played for me at DeMatha.

3 · A third requirement, and this is where some programs start to meet their downfall, is that once you get good assistant coaches, let them coach. Delegate authority to them. The refusal to do that is one of the largest single failings of most coaches. If you asked yourself the right questions before hiring your assistants—are they hard workers and professionally competent, are they loyal, do they have class, do they have the right disposition—and the answers all came up yes, then you know you have high quality assistants—so let them assist. My assistants know they have a responsibility all their own and that it is an integral part of our team and our success. I have one assistant in charge of pregame warm-ups, another responsible for coordinating our offense, another for supervising our defense, another in charge of rebounding. If you are afraid to delegate, you're doomed. The same is true if you delegate so much that you don't keep in proper touch with your operation. There's a middle ground and you have to reach it; it will be one of the reasons for the success which will follow.

4 Then there's motivation. If I had to pinpoint the one particular element of my own coaching method which

has helped us to succeed, that would be it: motivation. I don't claim to be any special basketball genius. I don't know everything there is to know about the sport. I'm sure there are a lot of coaches walking around who know more. There is a lot more to coaching and winning than mere technical knowledge, however. Joe Gallagher has a chapter in his book on this subject called "Going Beyond the Xs and Os," and that says it right there. There is so much more to basketball or football or any other sport than just drawing lines on a blackboard, or reading somebody's diagrams or theories about defense.

The game is still played by human beings. You can be the most brilliant technician in history, and your players the best-schooled ever in the technical points of the game, but your team isn't going to be a consistent winner if your players do not feel inspired to excel out of pride for both their team and themselves. When our players start out at DeMatha, I give each of them a description of what I want in them.

THE DEMATHA PLAYER

A DeMatha basketball player is a man with pride in himself as a student, an athlete and a member of the community. He, as a member of the basketball program, not only represents himself and his family, but also his fellow teammates and coaches. As our program continues to grow and prosper, he will constantly be in the eye of his fellow students and the general public. He shall be a leader and conduct himself in such a manner as to be praised, not as a basketball player, but more importantly as a man.

A DeMatha basketball player has goals for himself

as a student, player and a man. To attain these goals, he bases his life-style on hard work, 100 percent effort, sacrifice, sound effort, determination, punctuality and persistence. Just as these ideals will bring championships on the court, they will also reap rewards in the classroom and earn him greater respect as an individual.

A DeMatha player always has his head up; he looks his fellow man and the world in the eye. He is a class man in a class program. A DeMatha player always has his priorities in the proper order: God first, family second, school and studies third.

Congratulations and welcome to the team.

With my returning players, I hold individual conferences at the end of the season about what they should concentrate on over the summer and early fall to make the next season even better. I also get the comments and suggestions of each of my assistants in writing about every player. That's something I learned from George Allen when he was coaching the Redskins. George and I were at a party one night at the home of my sister, Clare Crawford-Mason. Clare has a rule for her parties: no sports talk. That night it looked as if that rule would be obeyed, because George and I were the only two sports people there, but we found our way out to the kitchen and talked sports anyhow. He told me that in matters of player evaluation and other related subjects if you want a truly candid opinion, get them to put it in writing. If they're willing to commit their comments to paper, then you'll know they really mean what they say.

I remember Bill Langloh's case. Bill was a tremendous

sophomore, but some of my assistants thought he was a little too slow to achieve the greatness that we wanted out of him, a condition which can sometimes be corrected. Because of those evaluations, I was able to call him into my office and tell him frankly, "Bill, everybody says you're half a step too slow. You'll be heading into your junior year next year and you'll want to go beyond that, on into college. And, naturally, you're going to want a scholarship, and go to a good school, so you'll have to increase your speed to pick up that half-step."

My players are never upset or panicky at that kind of comment because they know we run an objective program in which criticism is always constructive, never negative or personal. It is always done with one goal in mind: helping the boy and his team. Bill responded the way I knew he would: "What should I do to eliminate the slowness, Coach?"

I gave him his prescription: "You're going to have to jump rope a half-hour every day. You'll have to do crab runs an hour a day. You'll have to run the stadium steps every day." He did all those things all summer, and by September he *was* much faster. That's one of the reasons why he got a scholarship to the University of Virginia and became such a big star there. It wouldn't have done any good for me to have just said, "Bill, it's too bad, but you're half a step too slow for the big time," or to have told him the problem without also telling him how to correct it.

Sometimes I don't know how to correct a boy's problem. In that case, I'll find someone who does. Will Rogers had the right idea when he said, "Everybody is ignorant— only on different subjects." Coaches should never make the mistake of trying to make their players think they know all about everything. The players are aware that you don't, because you're a human being like the rest of them. They may lose respect for you if you try, and you can do them some real damage, even physical harm, if you try to give them wrong advice about some aspect of conditioning or treatment that you don't know enough about.

It happened in Adrian Dantley's case. We felt he needed to go on a weight program to increase his strength for his final year at DeMatha, but I don't pretend to know that much about weights—when I was an athlete, their use was relatively unknown. Instead, I went to some college weight instructors and asked them to put something together for him. I told Adrian I simply didn't know enough about weights myself. I had no intention of telling him something that might mess him up permanently, just because my ego might get in the way. It wouldn't have done either of us any good.

Trust in the coach is one vital element in motivating a player; he's got to know that he can believe you when you tell him to do something. Motivation is a tricky thing. Some players respond to one method, some to another. Adrian, for example, responded well to the sharp needle. I got on him pretty hard at times during our four years together, and I think he benefited from it. If he was having a poor game, I'd tell the team at halftime as I was looking down the stats sheet, "I see Beverly Dantley had two rebounds in the first half. That's very good, Beverly. Now see if you can go out in the second half with that really rugged determination and maybe you'll get two more rebounds in the second half. That will mean you'll have four rebounds for the whole game—Beverly." He would bristle at my calling him by a girl's name, but I did it because I knew he would still be bristling when the second half began—and when a guy with all his talent gets angry, look out.

Dantley remembers that treatment. He told a reporter not long ago, "Morgan wasn't afraid of me. When I was a ninth grader, he kept me in that gym for a week doing everything. Push-ups, running. He nearly killed me. It was what I needed. No man had ever stood up to me before. In four years, though, he never screamed at me or said a curse word. But he could get to you."

The year after Hawkeye Whitney graduated and headed south for stardom at North Carolina State, I had a special motivation challenge in Chris Gildea. I told him he would have to take up the rebounding slack now that Hawkeye was gone, but in training he looked awful. He wasn't doing anything right, and I knew something had to be causing it because he was just too good to be playing this poorly.

I called him aside one day and asked him what was wrong. He leveled with me completely, even though he was almost in tears, saying, "Last year I felt you were coaching me. This year you're just hollering at me."

I was delighted that he was so honest with me—and because of it, I knew then that Chris didn't respond to that kind of handling. As a result, I handled him a little more gently and he helped lead us to our undefeated season and the national championship.

I've always encouraged my players to be completely open with me and I promise that I will be with them. That way we help each other in a mature way, with no tender feelings hurt and no wrong ideas planted. Instead, we know we care for each other.

Pete Strickland, who later starred at Pitt, was a great player for us, but halfway through his senior year he had troubles. I called him to the office one day and said, "Pete, what's the problem?"

He told me, "Basketball is no fun anymore. I can't sleep. It's interfering with my classwork. I think you're asking too much of me. I feel that I have to carry the whole load."

So I said, "Pete, I want you to promise me something. I want you to promise me you'll go out there and just have fun. Have a great time. If we win them all, okay. If we lose them all, that's okay, too. It's still just a game, and I want you to just have a ball."

Well, he had a ball all right. From then on, he averaged twenty points a game, and we came from two games behind to win the Catholic high school championship for the Washington area. Then we beat Dunbar for the city championship at Cole Field House.

Those championships illustrate another of the motivational messages I pass on to my teams. Each year, usually during one of the five- or ten-minute sessions we hold in a classroom each day after practice, I hand out some words to help them over the rough spots they experience from time to time as high school students. Maybe the same words will come back to them later in life when they hit another rough spot, and maybe the advice will help then, too.

DON'T QUIT

When things go wrong, as they sometimes will,
When the road you're trudging seems all uphill,
When the funds are low and the debts are high,
And when you want to smile, but you have to sigh,

When care is pressing you down a bit—
Rest if you must, but don't you quit.

Life is queer with its twists and turns,
As every one of us sometimes learns,
And many a failure turns about
When he might have won had he stuck it out.
Don't give up, though the pace seems slow—
You may succeed with another blow.

Often the goal is nearer than
It seems to a faint and faltering man;
Often the struggler has given up
When he might have captured the victor's cup.
And he learned too late, when the night slipped down,
How close he was to the golden crown.

Success is failure turned inside out—
The silver tint of the clouds of doubt.
And you never can tell how close you are,
It may be near when it seems afar;
So stick to the fight when you're hardest hit—
It's when things seem worst that you mustn't quit.

Today's teenagers are just as smart as people of my generation were, and they're more mature. You hear a lot about drug problems and protests and all, but we had our problems, too, and that didn't mean we weren't decent people when we were in our teens. Today's generation is just as decent.

Because they've been brought up in a different era, though, with mass communications and advanced learning and teaching techniques, they seem to want to know the why behind our decisions, and there's nothing wrong with that. They don't resist, necessarily, or even complain, but they want to know the reasons for them. My own experiences with kids have proven to me that if you honor their curiosity, and deal with them on a respectful one-to-one basis when they're looking for those reasons, you'll get along with them, and they'll be better for it.

When Ron Satterthwaite was playing for us, for example, the team he was on was loaded with talent. He clearly was not going to crack that starting lineup even though he knew he was a good ball player, better than most and good enough to make the first string on almost any other high school team in America. One day at practice I took him off to the side and explained to him what he was up against, but I also pointed out to him why he had reason to feel good about this team and his part on it.

"You're going to be the most famous sixth man in America," I told him. "I want you to go home and tell your parents and the rest of your family, your girl friend and all your buddies and anybody else you want to, that I said you're going to be a key part of this team and that you're going to play a lot of minutes and have a lot of fun and success as the best darn sixth man ever.

"As proof of what I'm promising, let me tell you something else. You'll probably enter the game early, at some point in the first quarter. But if we're playing a game where you haven't been in yet and it's the end of the first quarter, I want you to stand up and tell me—and I'll put you in."

That's the way we worked it all year long, and Ronnie got a scholarship to William and Mary, as our sixth man, because he understood the situation and why things were the way they were. Ronnie's situation also illustrates another piece of advice we pass along to our players every year. We tell them not to try to figure everything out in one day or try to get everything accomplished all at once; they shouldn't become discouraged if they can't immediately see beyond a certain situation to the reason for it, or get down on themselves if the struggle seems to be taking longer than they expected.

I tell them the important thing is to do something every day, to work *consistently* toward their goal. It's amazing how much you can accomplish in life if nobody cares who gets the credit. And I tell them our rhyme to help them take things one day at a time:

"Inch by inch, life's a cinch. Yard by yard, it's really hard."

One more ingredient that's vital for any young person growing up, athlete or not, is the ability to determine who is influencing you. Are you listening to good people, associating with friends and elders who are not only fun to be with but can also help you head in the right direction? Or are you running around with a bunch of rowdies who pretend to be having more fun than anyone else simply because they're raising more trouble, the kind who suddenly and mysteriously drop out of sight after graduation and sometimes before? There are people in this world who can help you get where you want to go, and there are others who will keep you from getting there, and you have to recognize the winners and stay with them.

I tell my kids they don't even have to look outside their own homes to get some valuable help for their start in life. My father always drilled into me the importance of being yourself and of telling the truth, and my mother showed me her intense drive to succeed and her love of competition. Those things stuck with me and I've tried to pass them on each year to my history students and to my athletes. I tell our players, as every coach should, that they can get that same kind of help and healthy influence from their own parents and other adults, and they should be smart enough to make good use of the availability of that help.

During the course of my life and career, I've been fortunate to have had help too, from so many good people it would be hard to name them all.

Joe Gallagher was one of the first. We met when I was a teenager running around with his ballplayers and occasionally presenting a new challenge for him. He gave me my first coaching job, and it's no accident that we're still working together today in our Metropolitan Basketball Camp. Joe taught me the importance of being a gentleman as a coach, and of being gracious both in victory or defeat, no matter what the circumstances. After every game, win or lose, he has his players shake hands with each of the opposing team's players, and he does the same with the opposition's coach. I instituted the same practice as soon as I began coaching. I could write a whole book just on what Joe Gallagher taught me.

Jim Kehoe, whom I studied under at Maryland and who compiled an astounding record of success as Maryland's track coach and then put together its winning years in football and basketball when he became its athletic director, drilled into me the importance of developing efficiency, hard work and discipline in yourself before you can expect to develop it in your players. His approach to work was that if you have a job, get it done. Don't put it off, and don't do it halfway. Do it now, and do it right. He was a stickler for walking that straight line in everything.

Johnny Ryall was a good influence on a young man like me, not just because he was willing to give me money to buy baskets for our outdoor practice court at Saint Joseph's orphanage and to help individual needy boys, and not just because he helped to pay for the gym at Saint John's. It was because of his snowball philosophy of life. He used to tell me that if you helped someone, maybe they'd remember that when they got an opportunity, and they'd help someone, and so it would go—people helping people, all because you helped someone to begin with. It's a beautiful attitude, and one I've tried to practice myself and to foster in my students and players.

Ken Loeffler was a man willing to teach a lot about basketball to a young guy just starting out as a coach. As the head coach at LaSalle—and a strategic genius twenty years ahead of his time—he guided his team to the national championship and is now in the Basketball Hall of Fame. I moved many salt and pepper shakers around airport and restaurant tables with Ken. Later he went on to a brilliantly successful career as a lawyer, making him a champion in two different fields.

Ken was a brilliant innovator, the inventor of the 1–4 offense, some excellent practice routines, and the technique of showing one offensive set and then switching quickly into another. Ken was a vigorous preacher about what he called "positive turnovers." He always said too many coaches got hung up on trying to hold turnovers to a minimum. Ken said that was okay as far as it went, but it didn't go far enough. He used to tell coaches, "If your

team is not committing some turnovers, you're not playing basketball. I see coaches who are scared to press, afraid
to throw the long pass, all because they're afraid their team
might commit a turnover. If you're not making mistakes,
you're not playing."

Ken was the man who dreamed up the trick of running
the fast break down the side because everybody on defense used to concentrate on the middle of the floor, and
he wasn't above creating a few little stunts to help con the
officials into making calls his way. One trick, especially
before a big game, was to walk out to the official on the
floor just as the game was about to begin, point up into
the stands and say, "Can you wait just a minute? My cam-
eraman isn't quite ready." The official would look into the
seats and, sure enough, there would be a photographer
setting up his tripod to film the game. Then the photographer would wave that he was ready, and the official
would start the game.

The only thing wrong with that was that there wasn't
any film in the camera. Ken never had any money to buy
film, but the photographer wasn't up there for that anyhow. He was there so the officials would think the game
was being filmed—along with all their calls. It was Ken's
way of helping improve the officiating, or so he said. He
told me it was especially helpful on the road: When those
officials saw that movie camera up there, they really made
sure of their calls, thus reducing the number that might
have gone the home team's way.

Dean Smith is another innovator and another partner
in conversations that last on into the night. In fact, he may
hold the record. Back in the mid-1960s, when he was re-

cruiting Joe Kennedy and Brendan McCarthy from De-
Matha, he flew up from North Carolina one night to take
them and Kathy and me to dinner at Blackie's House of
Beef in Washington. Joe consumed two complete steak
dinners, I had the band play the Tar Heels fight song to
impress Dean and help the boys' cause with their recruiter,
then we took the boys home at a decent hour and went out
again, the three of us. We closed Blackie's at two in the
morning, then transfered to an uptown restaurant and
sat there talking basketball until past dawn. I took Kathy
home, she changed into her white uniform and went on to
her job as a nurse at George Washington University Hospital, and I changed and went out again to start a new day
at DeMatha.

Vic Bubas, highly successful as Duke's basketball coach
and now commissioner of the Sunbelt Conference, is another man you can learn from. He has always emphasized
to me the need for efficient organization of one's program
and how to achieve that. His simple three-point formula
for athletic success:

1. You have to get good players.
2. You have to keep them.
3. You have to coach them.

He especially made me aware of the need to get good
assistants. He used to tell me, "The ones you want are the
guys who want to become head coaches some day. They're
the only ones who make good assistant coaches."

Red Auerbach taught me one of the most valuable lessons
I've ever received, something both athletes and coaches
must learn if they want to be successful. Red talks about

"the feel of the game." One summer night we were playing a team of D.C. All-Stars at Jelleff's Branch of the Washington Boys' Club. For fifteen or twenty years now, Washington has had some of the finest high school basketball in the nation, so when you put the best players of that area on one floor, you really have something worth seeing. Courtside was packed (it was an outdoor court) and people were hanging in the trees, looking down from rooftops and leaning out of windows in nearby buildings. Red and Hot Rod Hundley, the West Virginia All-American and NBA star, were there, and so was Bud Millikan, then the head basketball coach at Maryland.

It was a sensational game, and we lost it in overtime. The next day, Red Auerbach came out to our Metropolitan Basketball Camp to speak, as he does every summer, and I asked him how he had liked the game, then waited for what I was sure would be a nice compliment from the great coach of the champion Boston Celtics. He didn't hesitate. "What did I think of it? It was a shame. You cost them that game."

I couldn't believe my ears. I thought we had done a great job just coming that close to winning against an All-Star team composed of that many great players, and I certainly didn't think the loss was my own fault. I asked him what he meant.

He said, "You lost the feel of the game. During that final timeout, you weren't talking about the things you should have been covering. You were talking about your offense, but you were getting beaten down at the other end. You were beginning to lose control of the boards, but you weren't talking about rebounding or boxing out. You were talking about what play to set up. It's simple. You lost the feel of the game."

I've never forgotten that.

These are the ingredients essential to building and maintaining a winning athletic program, based on my own experiences and those of people who have been around a lot longer than I have and made it.

The one most important ingredient, however—and one I must keep coming back to, even though I've talked about it a lot already—is the quality of your personnel. If you don't have good people, you're out of business. You must have boys who are more than just good ballplayers. They must be determined, hard workers, respectful to their superiors and their teammates and their opponents, who will work hard to develop themselves in *all* phases of life. I tell our players to do other things, develop other interests besides basketball: Read the news magazines and the editorial pages, go swimming or hiking, help around the house, get involved in the community—become a *total person.*

I tell those who want to prepare for careers in the pros: Set goals—but make sure they are realistic. Something not many of them realize is that there are over eight hundred thousand high school basketball players in this country, over sixteen thousand college players and fewer than three hundred professionals. Those are pretty staggering odds, so they'd better have something else to fall back on just in case the odds defeat them and they don't make it. The world is full of ex-athletes doing routine, uneventful and low-paying jobs just to exist, because they have not developed other interests and other skills. And even if you conquer those odds and make it as a professional, I add, some day you're not going to be able to play that game anymore, because your body won't let you. As Joe Gallagher tells his players, "After they take that ball out of your hands, what are you going to do for an encore?"

The Romans and the ancient Greeks emphasized the need for balance, control and discipline in life. Today, several thousand years later, they are still the things that contribute to success and happiness in this world. The advice of Saint Paul is right on the mark, too: "Be moderate in all things." Once you start doing anything to excess, it takes over, controls you—and defeats you.

John Wooden and I have had countless talks on this subject. We still have a lot of contact with each other, even though John has retired now from his brilliant career as head coach at UCLA. He's chairman of the Advisory Committee for the McDonald's High School All-American Game, and I'm chairman of its Selection Committee, so we see each other and talk to each other regularly. I've always felt encouraged, even flattered, that we both think the same way about so many of the key components of success, including the need for the right philosophy and the awareness that there should always be many dimensions to a person's life.

In his book, *They Call Me "Coach,"* John describes what he calls his "Pyramid of Success." He's built his career on it, a career that has encompassed ten national collegiate championships in twelve years—and the development of such stars as Kareem Abdul-Jabbar and Bill Walton. At the base of his "pyramid" are industriousness, friendship, loyalty, cooperation and enthusiasm. On the other levels leading to the top stand self-control, alertness, initiative, intentness, condition, skill, team spirit, poise and confidence. At the peak, above them all, is what he considers the final essential—competitive greatness. "Be at your best when your best is needed," John says. Champions must have "a real love of a hard battle."

And there is no reason why we can't all be champions, is there?

The Perfect Year

Things of great value come only after hard work.
                                                              —SOCRATES

DeMatha's world history teacher will tell you that the ancient Greeks emphasized excellence so much they even defined happiness as the full development of your ability along the lines of excellence. Coach Wootten agrees wholeheartedly with history teacher Wootten. His path to excellence involves a full measure of the painstaking, unglamorous side of coaching: organization, attention to detail, scheduling, the tedious repetition of teaching and explaining again, again, again. He blends that with his familiar stress on motivation, team attitude, self-discipline and decision. He breathes these virtues into his athletes individually and collectively, every day for four years.

By the time that fourth year begins, the athletes who are then seniors have the championship attitude: confidence in their own ability, confidence in their team, respect for each other, respect for their coach. Good things follow, and if the coach has taken the time and effort to line up a strong schedule against as many good teams as possible—and if fate smiles its widest grin—they might even go all the way . . .

At the end of the 1976/77 season, I knew we'd be ready for anybody the next year. It was ironic, because the '76/'77 DeMatha team had been only the second team since 1961 that had not won our conference championship. We had finished 29-4, however—certainly no embarrassment for any of us—and two of our four losses had been by a total of only four points. Although we hadn't had the dominating big man in the middle that year—and still wouldn't the next—everyone could see that this team was coming and would be ready to take on anyone next season. We wanted that conference title back.

The entire starting five was returning, along with most of our substitutes, eleven veterans in all. When you have that many returnees from a team that won twenty-nine games the year before, you know good things are going to happen, if you can avoid injuries.

As I've mentioned, each May I call the guys together who will be coming back, go over their coaching staff evaluation sheets and tell each player in private what his strengths and weaknesses are, what he should work on over the summer and what his role will be next season. The evaluation form grades the player on a scale of one to five in these categories:

Defensive ability—Stance, contesting the passing lanes, hedging, helpside defense, ballside defense, full-court defense, taking the offensive charge, anticipation of the next pass.

Shooting (minimum five hundred practice shots a day)
—Release, rotation, follow-through, shoulders square
to the basket, jump shot, foul shot, hook shot, drives,
power shots, baseline shots, shot selection.

The form also shows the player's stats for the season
just concluded, covering field-goal percentage, scoring
average, free-throw percentage, rebounding average and
the height of his vertical jump.

The player is given every opportunity to respond about
anything and everything, then leaves knowing what he
must do to become even better next year. He also knows
the rest is up to him. He's under no orders, only that com-
pelling force which comes from the pride of accomplishment.

I followed the same procedure that May, and the results
looked encouraging. I also encouraged them, as I do every
year, to play in the summer league composed of teams from
the Metro Conference. There's a team at each level—varsity, junior varsity and freshman—and that summer all three
of our teams won their league championships, without a
loss among them or an injury. A coach could be forgiven
if he got pretty excited about all that.

Then, in mid-August, we started on what would be one
of the greatest thrills any of us had ever experienced. We
had been scheduled to travel to mainland China to participate in an unprecedented series of basketball demon-
strations, but then Mao Tse-tung had died and, naturally,
the Chinese government asked us to postpone the trip. We
quickly found a substitute, however. The Organization of
American States asked us and Howard University of Washington to travel to Brazil on a goodwill tour, and we

jumped at the chance. It was the first time the OAS had ever sent any sports teams to South America. For fifteen days, over eighteen hundred miles, we traveled throughout Brazil by bus. We saw every part of Brazil, at every hour, in the city and the country, in its mountains and on its beaches. It was glorious.

I took all eleven veterans, and those coaches who refuse to let their teams travel out of town should have been with us and seen the fun and education our boys received from that experience. Joe Gallagher and I, and other coaches, have been criticized by some of our colleagues for supposedly making basketball too important and keeping our players from their studies. I feel sorry for coaches and administrators with that kind of reverse logic, but I feel even sorrier for their players. We schedule our trips in conjunction with weekends if they're during the school year, and the students never miss more than a day of school, two at the most. They take their books with them, and there are times when they know they have to study, especially with a history teacher as their coach to make sure they do it. I sometimes think our athletes get more studying done on those weekends than the athletes of the stay-at-home coaches do, and they certainly learn more, under proper supervision, about the world and the other people and places in it. What could be more educational than that?

Dutch Morley, our point guard on that team, kept a detailed diary on the trip, out of which eventually emerged a "Brazilian Journal" which illustrates the point better than anything I can say. It's all there, the sights and the sounds of discovery, the beautiful vision presented to us as we came down a mountain on the team bus, with the five o'clock sun just setting and saw Santos spread out below, the water from the Atlantic Ocean welling into the channels and streams on the outskirts of town; the lessons he learned about the people who seem so far away and yet are so close to us: "The 'North' in front of American is very important," he writes at one point, "because the Brazilians also consider themselves Americans."

The boys learned that American favorites are favorites in both Americas, North and South. Music, for instance. When meeting new friends in Brazil they often found their conversation turning to talk about groups and singers all of them knew. Led Zeppelin, James Brown, the O'Jays, the Eagles and Black Sabbath proved to be a language in common.

We played twelve games in Brazil, under international rules, and won them all, even with the greater amount of pushing and shoving allowed under those rules and some rather blatant home-team officiating. We had only one or two close calls. Even with liberal substitution and a slowed-down offense, we beat a few teams by forty points, another by seventy-seven and one by *ninety* (136–46).

By far our toughest game was in San Jose des Campos against a team whose star was a two-time Olympian. We had been warned it would be our most serious challenge, and the information was correct. After five minutes the score stood 15–12, DeMatha; after ten minutes, 25–21. They were staying right with us. The Olympian was six feet seven inches tall and an exceptional passer; he kept hitting the open man, and as a result his team played better as a unit than any other team we had faced. With two minutes left in the half, their players began to tire and our fresher substitutes ran off a 10–2 scoring streak that opened the gap to 38–31 at halftime, but the Brazilian team wasn't through. In the second half they kept "clawing and fight-ing," as Dutch puts it, and cut our lead to five points sev-eral times. They could never get any closer than that, though, and we managed to save the win, and our streak, 70–61.

We kept up our blitz during the rest of the schedule, even once when they threw in an extra game without telling us, causing us to play our eleventh game in thir-teen days, and those two days off consisted of an all-day bus trip each time. The surprise game was in Rio, and Dutch remembers it well in his journal:

> The ride to the game was about fifty minutes (from the hotel and) . . . the locker room was about two blocks away (from the gym) . . . We were very flat at the beginning . . . dead tired . . . They jumped off to an early lead and their biggest lead was 32–21 with about four minutes to play in the first half. They played a very deliberate ball control game and shot about 70 percent in the first half . . . With about six minutes left, we began to open up a little lead at 58–52 and were gaining momentum. Before we knew it, we were playing five-against-seven. The referees called three personal fouls and two technical fouls within thirty seconds . . . We walked off the floor and stood in a corner of the gym . . . Mr. Wootten talked to the referees . . . He said we would continue only if the refs agreed to stop cheat-ing, and they did. They actually admitted they were cheating and said they'd stop. By now it was 58–57. We were pretty well fired up so we did take command from there on in. The final score was 68–61.

All of us had a thrill awaiting us after that surprise game, though. The next day we went by bus to the top of Coronado Mountain in Rio to see the statue of Jesus Christ the Redeemer: 124 feet, 1,260 tons rising in inspiration and tribute from its base 2,300 feet above the city. Below was a widescreen view of all of Rio: mountains, beaches, forests, forty-story buildings and one-story huts. It was spectacular. The boys could never have gotten that sight staying at home.

After those fifteen days and twelve wins, we were still undefeated, and I had to wonder just how good we were. Our starters were awesome, as coaches and writers like to say, and our bench looked like it could wear anybody out. Our substitutes were better than the starting five on many good high school teams, and I knew what I had was my deepest team ever in a quarter of a century of coaching. It was going to take an outstanding team to beat us.

When September came, we had our annual opening meeting, when I talk to all the boys trying out for the team. I limit the meeting to fifteen minutes or so and tell them how many spots are open and what the younger players should be doing on their own until practice begins on November 8. I went over the schedule and handed out individual workout sheets which told the various players what they needed to do to build up their physical condition with weights and running and exercises. I insist on absolute top condition for every player. If it comes down to which team is in better shape, I tell our team, the worst DeMatha will do is tie, because nobody will ever be in better shape than the Stags—and very few will ever be in as good condition. This particular year I also mentioned that we had not won our conference championship the year before. I didn't dwell on it; I just reminded them.

As usual, I handed out one other piece of paper at that short meeting in September, too. It doesn't have anything to do with basketball, but it's a lot more important. It's an academic file. Each player is required to fill out a form every week for me, showing his grade for that week in each of his subjects. The teacher fills out the same kind of form once every three weeks, so the players know they have to give me the straight information. We stay on top of them academically all season long. Not only do students have to pass an entrance examination drawn up and administered by the Archdiocese of Washington to get into DeMatha (or into any Catholic high school in the metropolitan area), but unlike public schools in many parts of the country, our players must meet academic standards to retain their eligibility. If they don't, they're off the team. At many public schools, you can flunk your subjects and keep on playing. That's their business, but we don't hold with it.

After the forms were passed out, I took a minute to encourage the players, especially the new students, to be good members of the student body, to go see our football and soccer teams play in the fall and our other teams in the spring, then I dismissed everyone but the seniors. I held them back for a minute or two to go over the rules for recruiting; they were going to be blitzed like never before by scouts and coaches this year, and I wanted them to be prepared.

I usually schedule four scrimmages to start off the year, and this fall our opponents were Peary High School of Rockville, Loyola of Baltimore, T. C. Williams of northern Virginia, and Deep Creek High School of Norfolk. My assistants—Jack Bruen, Bernie McGregor, Perry Clark —and I thought we looked great in every one.

We opened the season at home against W. T. Woodson, another school in nearby northern Virginia, and won easily, 105–66, with what the *Washington Post* the next morning called "a tenacious man-to-man overplaying pressing defense and a world-class fast break offense." The *Post* said, "Before one could draw his eyes away from the action, the first quarter had ended with DeMatha out in front, 27–8." Twelve of our fourteen players had scored and four of them—Percy White, Dereck Whittenburg, John Carroll and Tommy Branch—had scored in double figures, Branch getting twenty-five.

For our second game, we traveled to Pennsylvania, a few hours from Maryland, to settle a score with Monsignor Bonner High. Not only had Bonner been one of the only four teams to beat us the year before, but that loss had snapped our winning streak at home after 115 straight. We hadn't lost a game at DeMatha since the first year of the Eisenhower administration, and Jimmy Carter was president when Bonner beat us—by one point. This time we were ahead all the way, by twenty at the half, and finished with a 75–59 win.

The victories kept coming, and so did the headlines:

DEMATHA COASTS PAST WOODSON, 105–66
BRANCH LEADS DEMATHA TO EASY VICTORY, 94–68
DEMATHA ROMPS

We breezed through our first nine games, including an eleven-point victory over the number-one teams in North and South Carolina and Kentucky. When we beat Shelby

County, the best Kentucky team, the Louisville *Courier-Journal* said, "Each substitute Coach Morgan Wootten sends into the game seems to be as good as the player he replaces." It was the second game of the evening that particularly interested me, however. Verbum Dei High School of Los Angeles had been picked to win the national championship and they were up against Kentucky's number seven team. They beat them, but only by one point. That set me thinking. We had been picked to finish second, and here we were beating the best Kentucky team by eleven and Verbum Dei had beaten the seventh best by only one. I wondered if that was significant.

That swing through North Carolina, South Carolina and Kentucky was made over a weekend, as usual, our boys missing only a Friday and a Monday from school, and when we came back home on December 22, it was time for a four-day break. I told them, "You're on your own. Get plenty of rest. Sleep all you want. Don't even pick up a basketball unless you feel like it. Have a great Christmas with your families, help out as the family gets ready for it and be a part of the fun and excitement, with your parents and the rest of the family. I'll see you on the twenty-sixth. Merry Christmas, fellas."

The day after Christmas we got together to run the turkey off—and followed that with two tough practices, to make sure we were still sharp and to allow enough time for all of us to enjoy Christmas week. Near the end of that week we traveled up into neighboring Pennsylvania again for a tournament in Johnstown, and for the first time ran into serious trouble.

Our opponent in the finals was Norwin High School. We had seen the Knights play earlier and our guys were a little too confident this time, yawning a bit, with the result that at the half we were losing by three points. Things got worse in the third period and by the start of the fourth quarter we were actually down by six.

Before that last quarter started, I told our team, "Okay, fellas, we have one quarter to go. We can play a lot better than we have been playing. But we have only one quarter in which to play championship ball. We're not going to try to get even all at once. That's the worst thing we could do. Instead, we're going to hit both boards. We're going to work the ball on offense. We're going to use good shot selection. We're going to hit the open man. We're not going to panic. We're going to nibble away at them." I was remembering Red Auerbach. The feel of the game.

Paul DeVito came out smoking and sank four jump shots from the perimeter, plus a free throw (he would have eighteen points for the game, half of them in the fourth quarter), but even with that, we were still losing 50–48. Then Tommy Branch converted a missed Norwin free throw into a basket at the other end to pull us even, and we were never behind after that. We went to our press, took the lead and finished with a 62–54 win and our seventh Johnstown tournament championship in eight tries. Once again our defense was one of the keys. Norwin committed twenty-four turnovers.

That game was a good thing for us. For the past couple of months our guys had been hearing and reading what a great team we were, and we needed a pressure situation like that, a game that went down to the wire, to sharpen us up. It was especially helpful that it came early in the season in a nonleague game. It developed the team's ability to handle the close games we knew were going to come later in the year, in our league and in the playoffs and tournaments which might follow. It was a maturing experience for our players, both individually and collectively, and they handled themselves well.

Then came January 2 and the start of our season in the Metro Conference. Our opponents were the Mackin Trojans, always a basketball powerhouse and a team gunning for us because we had beaten the Trojans three times the year before. To make them even hungrier, their coach, Steve Hocker, had played nine games against us as an athlete at John Carroll High, also in our conference, and we had beaten Carroll every time. He was looking for us with revenge in his eyes.

In the days preceding the game, one of his stars, Moe Young, a senior guard, said something which it was impossible for me to forget. Young told a reporter, "It's as simple as this: Beating them is our number-one priority. It's really hard to say how we feel. It's almost as if we have to do it, and believe me now's the time." It was the attitude every team would bring into its game against us. I told our players several times that season, "Remember one thing: We are the game of the year on everybody's schedule. Every team will take the court against us knowing that if it beats DeMatha it will have had a great year and achieved a memorable upset. We're going to have to be sharp and cool every time out."

Thirty-five hundred fans squeezed themselves into Catholic University's gym and another couple of thousand were turned away that night. Mackin went to a disciplined offense right away and stayed with it the entire first half. The Trojans shot an unbelievable 78 percent from the floor in the first half, many of their shots coming from fifteen to eighteen feet, they outrebounded us, even though we were taller, 27–24, and they scored forty-six points against us. With all that, the score at the half was 48–46, DeMatha. With Mackin playing as well as it possibly could, as well as any team could, we were still winning by two points.

We were composed during halftime. We've always been a strong second-half team, and we are always aware that our peak physical condition will start to work for us in the second half of any close game. All I told our boys was to keep on playing tough defense and, this half, to make it even tougher.

We went out, executed our offense when we had the ball and kept the pressure on when we didn't. Tommy Branch showed again what a great pressure performer he is. Dissatisfied with his first-half performance, he took the floor smoking in the third period, made eight out of nine shots, plus a free throw, and with those seventeen points we started to pull away. When a reporter asked him about that hot streak later, Tommy showed the kind of quiet confidence possessed by every great athlete. "When I get the ball in close," he said, "I don't think there's anyone who's going to stop me all the time."

We won the game, 100–90, and what pleased me most was the way we had stayed right in there during that first half against one of the most torrid scoring performances I've ever seen any team put on. When your opponent is shooting almost 80 percent and you're still winning, you have to feel good. I told the boys at the half that they were showing me a lot of character by doing that. Then the second half pretty much took care of itself, with a lot of help from Tommy Branch.

After the game Steve Hocker said what was on a lot of people's minds. "One sentence," he said. "I can sum it up in just one sentence. They just wore us down. Their depth got to us." That great bench of ours which had performed so well during our trip to Brazil was flexing its muscles, and as the season wore on, they played more and their confidence blossomed; they just kept getting better and better. No doubt about it, we were a team destined for great things if we could avoid injury.

Mackin was a mighty big win in a very big game for us, and we kept rolling. Next was Eastern, a Washington public school. After leading by thirty points at one stage, we finished on top, 78–56. Our half-court press was working like a charm and we stole the ball twenty-nine times. Twelve of our players scored. When the officials called a technical foul on Eastern at the start of the second half for being late on its return from the dressing room, I turned it down. The officials couldn't believe me, but I told them, "I would never want to win a game on a call like that." Tommy Stinson covered the game for the Washington *Star* and in his article the next day, he said, "It was the only thing DeMatha gave Eastern all night."

We overwhelmed Carroll High, 100–37, in a league game, with Carroll committing thirty-two turnovers against our swarming man-to-man defense. With five minutes to play, our junior guard, Dereck Whittenburg, made the most exciting play of the game when he took the ball on a fast break and scored with a two-handed reverse stuff. He got a standing ovation—at DeMatha.

It wasn't anything new for Whit. He's only six feet tall, but he can jump as if he were seven feet. Whit's one of the few guys his height—high school, college or pro—who can slam dunk, including some dunks you wouldn't think possible even by much bigger men. Among the dunk competitions he's won was one against two of the best ever, Eugene Banks and Albert King, when they were high school seniors and Whit was only a sophomore. He was mature about it too, even as a high school kid. "I know the fans want me to do it," he says, "so I try to give them what they want to see." How does he do it? He's talented and agile, has tremendous jumping ability—and it doesn't hurt that his second cousin is NBA star David Thompson.

We kept on winning and headlines kept on coming:

> DEMATHA'S DEFENSE IS TOO MUCH FOR EASTERN
> DEMATHA'S 'NO-NAMES' MAY BE BEST
> DEMATHA KEEPS ROLLING ALONG
> DEMATHA TROUNCES ST. JOE
> DEMATHA IS JUST TOO DEEP FOR ST. JOHN'S
> GONZAGA IS DEMATHA'S 20TH VICTIM

After we beat Saint John's, 68–57, Billy Barnes, one of its stars, was asked how good our team was. "Good?" he asked. "Did you see them in the first half? They are so strong and deep, it's hard to describe. Yeah, they are as good as people say."

After the Gonzaga game, 84–56, the Eagles's coach, Dick Myers, told reporters we were the greatest high school team he had ever seen, and I had to keep reminding our players not to let it go to their heads. We were an exceptional ball club, but we had to prove it every game. And one of the real tests was coming up next.

By now people were rating us ahead of Verbum Dei as the best high school basketball team in America. Maybe Wootten's going to get his first undefeated season, they said, and the players were even open and confident enough to tell the writers they wanted to go undefeated for me. But there stood Mackin, again, even thirstier for revenge than before, and as if that weren't enough of a danger, the game was for the Metro Conference championship. Whoever won was still going to have to face Good Counsel in the finals, but they would be no problem. Mackin was the threat.

The setting was the same, and so was the pressure: Catholic University, packed again with a turnaway crowd. The start of the game had to be delayed twenty minutes because of the traffic jam outside. There were live television reports from courtside. By now people were coming out to see us not just to see us win and for our ability, but for our excitement and the way we played. We were proving ourselves not only a great ball club but one with charisma, a team with personality. In return, like all great teams, we responded with a quality performance.

The early going was tough, though. Steve Hocker's Trojans leaped out to the lead, 6–4, after an eighteen-foot jump shot by our old friend, Moe Young, before our players got down to serious basketball and outscored Mackin, 20–10. That gave us the lead, 24–16, at the end of the first period and at halftime we were leading by seven points.

The Trojans were far from through, though. Mackin came out with real intensity at the start of the third period with heavy pressure on defense, and when Kenny Payne and Moe Young made long jump shots, and Richard Crooks, who wound up as the game's high scorer with twenty-one points, hit three free throws, the game was suddenly tied, 43–43, with four minutes and one second left in the period.

We took a deep breath, and our scorers got hot again, running off a streak the way we had done so often that season when we needed the points. We outscored our opponent, 11–3, in the last four minutes of the third quarter and were home free. We won, 82–74. Steve Hocker threw every defense he could think of against us in that game—full-court press, half-court press, man-to-man, 2–1–2 zone, box-and-one, triangle-and-two—but it still couldn't stop us.

I had been confident it wouldn't, not with our experienced personnel. They recognized defenses quickly and made the appropriate adjustments. All of our players, individually and as a team, adapted as quickly as a lot of college teams. When they spotted the other team's defense, they knew right away what offense to run against it, and if the other team switched defensive alignments, as Mackin kept doing, the DeMatha offense switched offensive formations. Our guys always knew what they were doing out there.

By this, I mean not just the best players, but all of them. We were, as the press said, a "no-name" team. We did not have one dominant star, or even two. Our players didn't care who got the credit or who the high scorer was as long as they won the game. Our high scorer for the game was Joe Washington with only fourteen points. DeVito and Branch had thirteen each, and Chris Gildea had twelve. We had shot 51 percent from the floor as a team, even including the third string.

Two of the real heroes all season long were two of our lowest scorers in the game: Dutch Morley and Sidney Lowe. They always kept our offense flowing, played tough defense and contributed enormously to our wins every time, but they didn't care how many points they had and how much glory came their way. They played for their team, not for themselves. In that second Mackin game, Dutch and Sidney combined for only nine points—but ten assists. And, as the Washington *Star* pointed out, nine points "wasn't too bad considering they played most of the game thirty feet away from the offensive basket."

Now we had twenty-two wins. Good Counsel fell as expected, and the number was twenty-three, and we became the Washington area Catholic champions again, for the fourteenth time in sixteen years. That brought us to the next roadblock, Dunbar of Washington, which had won the city public school title the week before. Dunbar had a winning streak of its own going at nineteen straight and had lost only once all year, and now the Crimson Tide was itching to knock us off. It would be Dunbar, the public school champ, versus DeMatha, the Catholic school champ, for the city title.

It was not the first time our two teams had found themselves in this kind of a setting. Two years earlier, we had played Dunbar for the city title and lost, and Dunbar had been voted the nation's top team. Now here we were again, with the Stags trying to get what Dunbar had won two years ago.

The game, played at Maryland's Cole Field House in front of more than ten thousand fans, was a tough back-and-forth battle which gave us a real scare until the fourth quarter, when we were finally able to pull away. We won that game, and most of the particulars themselves aren't that important, but there was one strong lesson in it for us and for every basketball team. We outscored Dunbar in the final quarter 23–18, mostly on the strength of thirteen free throws in seventeen attempts. Coaches put a great deal of emphasis on foul shooting, at least the successful coaches do, and fans and reporters sometimes think we're over-stating the case. Here was a situation, though, in which our ability to make free throws—under pressure—helped De-Matha win the city championship. We were given thirty shots from the foul line, because we were converting one-and-one opportunities, and we made twenty-five. Dunbar made only five of twelve, giving us a twenty-point advantage on them in free throws. The final margin of that game was eight points, 63–55. That says it all on the importance of free throws.

After every practice, we have a drill. Each player shoots forty free throws. If the team percentage of those 480 free throws is not at least 70 percent, I line everybody up at the foul line and have them run "double suicides" from one foul line to the other, back and forth, as fast and as hard as they can. They'd rather be accurate from the foul line than do that. It's not just punishment for missing, it's a way of making them shoot a lot of free throws while you stand around or go out in the hall and bat the breeze with your assistants. The players have to be shooting them for a rea-son, under some kind of pressure, because that's the way they'll be shooting them in a game. Those double suicides aren't fun, but they serve their purpose. Sometimes they win games for you—even city championships.

So now we were conference champions, city champions —for the thirteenth time in eighteen years—ranked number one in the country and still undefeated, 24–0. It had been a dream year so far, but there was one more hurdle to con-quer, the annual Alhambra Invitational Tournament in Cumberland, Maryland, which is like the World Series of basketball for Catholic high schools. Cumberland is only two hours by car from us, and we had won the Alhambra four times before, but this short trip was going to be one of the most important journeys any DeMatha team had ever made.

The pressure was building and so was the publicity. Stories about the team and its coach appeared in papers all over the country. Austin Carr, a member of the Cleveland Cavaliers in the NBA and a star at rival Mackin in his high school days, told a Florida paper, "You can have a better team than DeMatha and you won't beat them. The man (Wootten) must have invented basketball."

North Carolina coach Dean Smith echoed the Wootten philosophy. "It's not that Morgan understands basketball that much. I mean he does. I learned the 'North Carolina' zone trap defense from him. But his real asset is his ability to work with kids and develop them into fine human beings. His players are always outstanding people."

Adrian Dantley told a reporter about Wootten, "They (area kids) respect his ability as a coach, but they admire his devotion to mankind." And the reporter added, "Wootten turned him into a student—a fact evidenced by his 3.2 grade average at Notre Dame."

Dick Heller wrote a prominent feature in the Washington *Star* with a big picture of Wootten talking to his team during the Gonzaga games, with a headline reading:

DEMATHA: The Years and the Faces Change,
            But the Wootten Method Remains

Reports have it, Heller said, that the first two words Wootten learned to say as a baby were "teamwork" and "balance." It might be a "no-name" team, he noted—no Bob Whitmore, James Brown, Adrian Dantley, Kenny

Carr or Hawkeye Whitney to operate as superstar—but that famous DeMatha teamwork and balance kept winning in the Wootten tradition.

College recruiters calling Morgan that season were made even hungrier than usual reading all that press and witnessing the team's continued success. They kept asking him who his best player was. Wootten's answer always surprised them: "I don't have any."

In that *Star* article, two of those "no-names," Joe Washington and Dereck Whittenburg, spoke out on the subject of teamwork and the ability to overcome the odds through an unselfish attitude.

"Do I wish I was playing some place where I could average twenty-five points?" Washington, senior guard and Most Valuable Player in the Alhambra Tournament the year before, said. "Not very much. DeMatha is the best place for me. Dereck works just as hard as me, and he deserves his chance. I knew things were going to come out this way on this team, although sitting on the bench so much was a little hard to accept for a while. I don't think my low statistics will discourage the college recruiters. They know I've only been playing half the time. They know I have the ability to be a great player."

To this, Whittenburg, the master of the slam dunk and a junior, added, "I don't mind not starting until my time comes. Joe's got to start, he's a senior. This will help me. Next year I'll be starting and somebody else will be behind me and I'll understand how he feels. Yeah, I wonder what might happen to me at another school, but it's always been DeMatha for me. I read some clippings about Hawkeye a few years ago, and he had some things to say about DeMatha and education that made sense to me."

Even articles about other people kept making mention of DeMatha. A story from Raleigh, North Carolina, quoted Hawkeye Whitney about growing up as one of thirteen children in the ghetto. "I was lucky," he said. "I was blessed with a gift to play basketball and the right

143

kind of guidance when I needed it. Otherwise, I'd be on the streets now." The first time Whitney received "the right kind of guidance," at least in basketball, may have been when his coach at Johnson Junior High in Washington, John Garner, urged him to attend high school at DeMatha. Hawkeye's brothers and sisters chipped in to make it possible.

"I came from a Baptist upbringing," Hawkeye said, "and when he brought it up I told him I didn't think I wanted to go to a Catholic school. But after he explained how it could benefit me academically and in basketball, I wrote a letter to Coach Wootten."

Then Whitney told how it was to be an athlete under Wootten: "I never met a man like Coach Wootten. He never let me take a wrong turn. I wasn't allowed to roam the halls or cut class. He forced us to face our problems instead of running away from them. And he taught us the value of commitments: Always be early, never be late. We could relate to him, yet he earned our respect."

The stories, the film features on television, the radio reports, they all kept coming, but newspaper stories can't play your games for you. The Alhambra was still to come and Wootten and his athletes knew they were going to need all the help they could get. Consequently, every parent of every player made the trip to Cumberland and stayed for the entire tournament. That's what's meant by "being a part of the DeMatha family."

The tournament started, with DeMatha's undefeated record and number-one national ranking on the line on every play. DeMatha's first game was against Cardinal Gibbons High, Baltimore's city champions. Cardinal Gibbons had survived one of the most rugged schedules in the school's history, but it did them no good against the "no-names": Dematha seventy-seven, Cardinal Gibbons fifty-four. Twenty-five wins.

The next game against Father Judge High School of

Philadelphia looked to be harder, when the Crusaders went to the stall and wound up leading at the end of the first quarter, 8–7. DeMatha, though, kept its poise and broke things open with a blistering second quarter. The Stags outscored their opponents, 24–4, went into the dressing room with a 38–20 lead and were never in trouble the rest of the way. The final score was 63–40. Twenty-six.

Now it was time for the final game of the tournament, the biggest game for DeMatha since the famous Power duel of 1965. This was what was on the line: the prestigious Alhambra championship, the national championship and the coach's first undefeated season. And the team the Stags had to beat to make all this come true was Mackin, for the third time that year and the sixth time in two seasons. DeMatha had so many things working in its favor, but Mackin had one thing working in its own: the law of averages. Mackin was too talented a team to keep getting beaten.

As the two teams took the floor on that March evening in 1978, the words from one of Morgan Wootten's messages stuck in many of the DeMatha's players' minds. It was a composition called "How We Defeat Ourselves" by Sidney J. Harris, and certain underlined passages dealt with what an athlete must do when the heat is turned on.

"I think," one of those passages said, "that in the ultimate crisis, the real champion forgets himself entirely and concentrates with passionate ferocity upon his object." Another said that the greatest instinct in a champion is "the instinct for perfection—a perfection so exquisite in itself that it obliterates the man who is achieving it."

But the one part that was strongest in the minds of DeMatha's Stags that night, because it typified the Wootten message, was the line which read, "I am convinced that it is temperament, more than talent or brains, that determines whether we are self-fufilling or self-destroying." DeMatha intended to be fulfilled that night.

The guys were good and loose at the hotel, not cocky, just confident, the way a coach wants his team before a big game. When I saw how they felt, I felt the same way. Before leaving the hotel I packed a bag with a change of clothes because I fully expected to get thrown into the shower after the game.

You couldn't have asked for more from a basketball contest. It was another knock-down, drag-out fight between two outstanding teams, slugging it out toe-to-toe. By halftime the lead had changed hands six times and the score had been tied eight times, and we were behind by a single point. I told our players in the dressing room during the intermission, "Mackin is playing a great game, but so are we. And we know we're in better shape and have better substitutes. We're going to wear them down in the second half."

I remembered the words I had said the night before, after the semifinal game, when I had told our players they had one more night to keep in training, one more time to make sure they got a great night's sleep, and then they'd be able to remember the next twenty-four hours for the rest of their lives. I had told them they would want to be able to say they were totally prepared, and added, "You're going to be able to stay up late a whole lot of nights the rest of your life, but I just don't think tonight should be one of them." Because they set their own rules and their own curfews, they could have ignored my advice that night before Mackin, but they didn't. They all went to bed early, passing up the tournament's big dance.

We went out at the half, confident we could take it all, even though we were behind, 35–34. As we left the dressing room for the last two quarters of basketball that year, our men were yelling to each other, "Hit those boards! Let's go out in style!" It was exactly what I had come to expect of them in a situation like that.

We did go out in style, and just the way we thought we would: wearing Mackin down. Tommy Branch, who was later voted the tournament's Most Valuable Player award, scored six points in the first two minutes of the third quarter, was forced to sit out a few minutes with a twisted right ankle, then came back and made a four-footer which put us ahead by ten points with eight minutes to play. That sealed the game, and all our dreams came true: 74–64, DeMatha. Twenty-seven wins. The Alhambra, the national championship and the undefeated season.

Other dreams came true as well. As in the previous seventeen seasons, all eight seniors won full four-year college scholarships:

Dutch Morley—University of Maryland
Joe Washington—Colorado
Paul DeVito—Jacksonville
Chris Gildea—New Hampshire
Tommy Branch—Old Dominion
Mark Bruce—Wofford
Mike O'Driscoll—Wofford
Anthony Washington—Saint Francis of Pennsylvania

The messages poured in—letters, telegrams, greeting cards—from friends, associates, fellow coaches and strang-

ers. *Basketball Weekly*, the bible of the sport, made it
official with a long story under the headline which said
it all:

DEMATHA WINS NATIONAL PREP CHAMPIONSHIP

Morgan Wootten was voted Coach of the Year by the
national association of high school coaches, and, in the
kind of recognition which always pleases him most, was
saluted for his work off the court as well. The Washington *Star* was one of those rendering such a salute. On its
editorial page, that space reserved for such weighty
matters as war and peace, politics and inflation, the *Star*
ran a tribute titled simply, "DeMatha's Morgan Wootten." It likened the Wootten philosophy to Voltaire's:
"We must cultivate our garden."

The *Star* said, "Mr. Wootten has been able to function
as a teacher in the fullest sense. The youngsters who have
played under him . . . have been well tutored in values
and priorities as well as the way the basketball bounces."
It quoted Dick Heller: "Any athlete lucky enough to
play for Wootten knows that he had better put schoolwork and respect for teammates and teachers ahead of
sticking a ball into a basket."

The *Star* editorial concluded, "A good many young
Washingtonians have reason to be grateful that he has
cultivated his garden at DeMatha."

Morgan Wootten and DeMatha were featured on the
sports page of *Time* magazine in its issue of March 20.
To be even more accurate, they *were* the sports page.
Even though the NBA regular season was grinding toward its conclusion, baseball's spring training was well
under way and the pro golf tour still operating, *Time*'s
only sports article that week was about the Stags and
their coach, Morgan Wootten. Bob Whitmore told *Time*,
"The one outstanding quality Morgan has is his hon-
esty. When you are streetwise like I was, you learn to
read that."

Sid Catlett spoke up, too, giving Morgan credit for turning his life around. In that *Time* article, Catlett, who had been fatherless since he was three, said, "In my neighborhood I could have gotten into all kinds of trouble. Morgan could be a friend, coach or manly role model, depending on what was needed at the time. He was a vital influence in my life."

And Dereck Whittenburg, who had jumped *over* the referee, with the ref standing straight up, at the buzzer ending the perfect season, added: "I know I'll make something out of my life if I stick with the work now. Morgan will see to it."

Athletics and Academics: Speaking Bluntly

If you hoot with the owls at night,
You cannot soar with the eagles at dawn.
—A DeMatha slogan

The Wootten approach to basketball carries over into many other areas of life as well, and Wootten has never been afraid to voice his opinion on some of the crucial questions that confront young people and their parents today. I sat down with him one day and discussed some of them.

Q. *Morgan, what do you feel is the greatest need in American education today?*

A. Discipline. Our young people are being badly cheated by timid "educators," people who don't have the courage to enforce discipline, educators who are afraid of parents, afraid of school boards, afraid of community pressures. They'll do anything not to rock the boat. They pass students to the next grade when the kids aren't qualified to be passed. Most of all, they will not give their students the one thing they're crying for: discipline. They're *begging* for it.

Q. *You're from the school of coaching which says you have to have discipline to be successful.*

A. Absolutely. No question about it. The teachers and coaches who are respected are disciplinarians first of all. They're fair, they let you know where you stand, they make sure you follow reasonable rules. They don't let you walk over other people, they don't let you infringe on the rights of others, and if you have a penalty coming, they make sure you pay the price because that's just the way it is in our world.

Q. *The lack of respect for authority, and the lack of discipline which results, was unusually serious during the era of the Vietnam protests. You think it's still a serious problem?*

A. Yes, sir. Certainly. There are still far too many school systems which are badly infiltrated by people who don't care about our kids. They are content to get by, at any price, to give the kids what they think they want, not what *you* know they *need*. That's a very harmful attitude toward our society, and toward our children, yours and mine. Those people don't belong in teaching or in coaching if they are not going to have the courage to be disciplinarians and to be fair. You can't let students simply "do their thing," all on their own. And they don't want to, anyway. That attitude was a loser long before that awful expression became popular, and if you raise children by that attitude the kids become losers themselves. That's where you're cheating them. Kids don't want that. Instead, they want you to be interested in them and to discipline them.

They want you to respect them and to be able to respect you in return.

Q. *How do you see this lack of discipline on the basketball court?*

A. You play teams and hear their teenage players using lousy language and displaying absolutely pitiful conduct on the floor and giving out a lot of cheap talk. They make it easy for us to beat them because they never reach their potential. They're too busy doing everything but playing basketball.

Q. *You hear a lot of teachers complain about how hard it is to maintain discipline in the classroom. How do you handle this problem as a teacher?*

A. It's never a problem for me. I start off each class on the first day of school by saying, "Gentlemen, my name is Mr. Wootten. I'm your world history teacher and we're going to have a great year together. Your homework for tonight is . . ." Right off the bat they know who's boss and we're going to work hard. But they also know they have a strict, fair teacher and their year with me will be enjoyable and productive. So discipline has never been a problem in my classes.

Q. *But don't you ever have some clown who starts acting up? What do you do then?*

A. Oh, sure. But it won't happen more than once or twice the whole year in any class of mine, because of what I do the first time it pops up. I'll call the troublemaker up to the front of the room and say to the class, "Gentlemen, I invited Jimmy to come up front and stand here before you so he could get some attention. That's why he was acting up in his seat. He's trying to get your attention. But it's much easier to have him come up here and stand here so all of you can look at him and give him the recognition which he obviously needs very badly.

"Now, Jimmy, if you really have to have recognition, there are a lot of ways you can get it. You can make a fool of yourself in class, the way you've been doing just now. Or you could jump out that window over there. Everybody would be sure to notice you then. But I hate to see you embarrass yourself or get hurt jumping through windows. You're too good a person to have to use those means of getting recognition. Everybody likes recognition, including me. But there are better ways of getting it, and those ways can help you instead of hurting you. You can get recognition by being an outstanding student, or by being an athlete, or by doing both. Or working on the school paper or singing in the choir. The best way of all is to be a person of high quality. That's the greatest recognition any of us can get for ourselves. I didn't make you come up here to embarrass you. I did it to show you there are better ways of winning recognition than the path you've started down. So get smart right now and choose a more intelligent way. Doesn't that make sense, Jimmy?"

The student will always agree. Then I'll point out that everything I've just said applies to everyone in the class, not just to Jimmy. And I won't have any more fooling around in that class the rest of the school year.

Too many teachers are spending 90 percent of their time on matters of law and order. They're too busy to do any teaching. If they get the roll taken and there aren't any fights, then it's been a successful period. And the administrators down in the front office don't even want to hear about it.

I don't want that for my kids. My students, and every

teacher's students, deserve more than that, and at DeMatha they get it. By the end of the year, I want my kids to believe that I really care for them, that I had their interests at heart, that I know each of them as a person. I also want to feel that they were interested in the course and got a lot out of it, learning from me not just about history but about life.

Q. *How does this kind of attitude by school officials affect athletic programs, or does it have any effect?*

A. Yes, it does. There are many administrators who would cut back on athletics. They don't want too much competition in school life. Competition is bad for Johnny. They don't want to have to worry about crowd control at games. No competition makes everything easier for them. So they cut back on athletics if they can, again thinking in terms of their own convenience and not about what the kids need and deserve.

Q. *What about your trips? How do you answer those who say high school teams shouldn't travel?*

A. Taking your players on a trip once in a while, under close supervision, can be at least as beneficial as what they learn in the classroom, sometimes more. I've already discussed this matter some in reference to our trip to Brazil, but I want to bring up another example, closer to home. We were canceled out of a tournament in Winter Park, Florida, because the executive secretary of the Florida chapter of the National High School Athletic Association forbids Florida's high school teams from traveling outside the state or inviting out-of-state schools to play there unless they are association members. DeMatha doesn't belong to that association because it's mostly for public schools, and many big city school systems don't belong. Those that do, including the public schools in Maryland, often have a "friends and neighbors" policy under which out-of-state schools, even those not belonging to the national association, can be invited into the state as friends and neighbors, with the visiting school returning the favor the next time. That's what we were going to do. Our boys would have gotten to see central Florida and, more important, the next year, we were going to have the Winter Haven school visit DeMatha and Washington, D.C., only ten or fifteen minutes away. We would have shown them the White House, the Capitol, all the sights, and they could have met their senators or congressional representatives in their offices on Capitol Hill. It would have been the chance of a lifetime, but the Florida students were denied the opportunity by their own state executive secretary. His explanation was that it was against the rules, but the rules provide the "friends and neighbors" exception to avoid discriminating against nonmember schools. In this case it wasn't DeMatha that was discriminated against as much as it was his own Florida students.

Q. *Let's talk basketball for a minute. The practice of "taking the charge," which you've discussed earlier, has been criticized as too dangerous physically and not even good basketball. Yet you developed this tactic and your teams have become famous for it. How do you answer its critics?*

A. Johnny Herbert and I designed that technique because of a simple fact of life in basketball: You can prevent your opponent from scoring by blocking his path to the basket. It works. As far as any physical risk is concerned, there isn't any if you teach the right way to do it. You have to teach the kids how to fall: on their shoulders and the back of their arms, making sure they give at the moment of contact and have their knees bent ahead of time. *Taking* the charge isn't wrong. What's wrong is *faking* the charge. That's when you can get hurt. There's even an offensive value in encouraging your players to take the charge. It helps to teach your players to keep control of themselves and the ball when they're shooting so as to avoid the opponent who may be trying to line himself up to take the charge. It makes them "high jumpers" instead of "broad jumpers" when shooting. It's valuable and it's safe and it's effective, but your players have to do it right, and that means you have to teach it right.

Q. *Each year you let your team make its own rules for that season. How does that work?*

A. When we start practicing in early November, I tell the players it's their team, so they make their rules, but they'll have to obey their own rules. They decide whether to have a curfew on the night before a game, whether to forbid smoking during the season, questions of that kind. The rules will be theirs, but they know I'm the enforcer.

Q. *Do other coaches let their teams make their own rules?*

A. No, I don't think so. I don't know of any.

Q. *Has it been that successful? Does it always work?*

A. Yes, it's worked out fine over the years. There was one exception, though, but that wasn't the fault of the system or the players. It was my fault. We had just finished third in the Alhambra tournament up in Cumberland one year, but we still had the Knights of Columbus tournament to go and a date with Mackin and Austin Carr. Our players decided to set a 3:00 A.M. curfew to allow a few hours of celebrating our third place that evening. Since we didn't get back to the hotel from the game until almost midnight, I thought 3:00 A.M. was a reasonable hour under those conditions. However, I reminded the team that we had Mackin and the K of C tournament coming up, "so any player who breaks the curfew you've just set will be kicked off the team." That's where I made a serious mistake.

About five minutes after three, Kathy and I were sleeping when she heard a noise down the hall. I climbed out of bed and opened the door, and there were Sid Catlett and Billy Hite walking down the corridor. They'd broken the curfew, by only five minutes, but they'd broken it. I told the team at breakfast and made it clear: Catlett and Hite were through for the year.

During the two-hour drive back from Cumberland to Hyattsville, I was aware that I'd cut off my nose to spite my face. How could I get us out of the dilemma I'd gotten us into? It took a lot of serious thought, then I devised my solution. I told the team in a meeting that I had overstepped our arrangement. I had *set* the penalty instead of merely enforcing it. I was playing God by deciding myself *ahead of time* what the punishment should be and whether they should even *be* punished. I hadn't asked for any explanation. I had just flat kicked them off the team. I shouldn't have done that, and I admitted it to the team. I told them that Sid Catlett was a senior with three hundred college offers. "If my punishment sticks," I told the team, "about half of those colleges are going to think he's a bad person, even though we all know he isn't. So, in fairness to Sid, I'm admitting my own mistake and letting him back on. And Billy, you're lucky Sid is a senior. You're only a sophomore and I'd let the penalty stick in your case because it won't affect your college future, but I can't apply a double standard. I have to treat both of you equally, so you're back on the team, too."

Coaches—and teachers—shouldn't say, "Here are the rules—one, two, three—and here are the penalties—one, two, three." Good disciplinarians don't mention penalties, they are implied. Our teams don't set penalties, they set only the rules, and we assume everybody's going to keep them. Each case must be judged on its own merits. It was all a mistake—mine—and I learned from it. If anybody deserved to be punished for doing something wrong, it should have been me. Sid and Billy showed through the rest of their careers at DeMatha—and Sid at Notre Dame and Billy at North Carolina—what great people they are. And it turns out they even had a legitimate excuse: They had a flat tire. I hadn't even thought to ask. By the way we won the K of C tournament.

Q. *You haven't made that mistake again?*

A. No, but now that you mention it, I made a similar mistake years before that, this time in the classroom. I was a young history teacher at Saint John's and we were talking one day in class about Hammurabi—"the great Assyrian king." One of the students claimed that our textbook said he was a Babylonian. I said no, he was an Assyrian. When I got home that night, I checked the book. The kid was right. The next day, I asked Brother David on the teaching staff how to correct my mistake without costing myself some credibility with my students. He gave me the solution. I deliberately renewed the conversation in front of the class, and when the student repeated his statement that our textbook said Hammurabi was a Babylonian, I answered, "Oh, you mean *that* Hammurabi."

The class broke up over it. After the laughter died

down, I followed up by saying, "Let me tell you something. It's incredible to me that I made a mistake like that, and only one student challenged me. Where were the rest of you? You mean you're going to sit there and let me tell you things that aren't true and only one guy is going to pick it up?"

It worked so well, and proved so effective, that I now use that tactic on purpose. I'll deliberately make a mistake and see if the students call me on it. If they don't, I get on them about it. It encourages the students to think for themselves and to question people and their information, not just in class but in the world. Don't swallow everything that is fed to you without making sure it's right information. I reminded them of another of my favorite sayings:

When all else fails—think.

Q. *You coach at a Catholic school, so your situation is different, but in public schools, is there room for religion in athletics?*

A. You don't have to listen to my answer on that question. Bud Wilkinson gave the answer years ago when he said, "Show me a young athlete with a spiritual commitment and I'll show you a winner." You don't have to espouse a particular religion, but in my opinion coaches should definitely encourage a religious attitude, meaning an attitude of love, respect and brotherhood, all the virtues which Christ preached to us about. You cannot find a basketball team where the players feel this way which doesn't win. That's a spiritual commitment, and not even Madelyn Murray O'Hare can get that declared unconstitutional. It's the same attitude which John Kennedy showed at the end of his inaugural address when he said that "here on earth . . . God's work must truly be our own." Same thing. It's the kind of outlook I have in mind when I talk about the need to have *good people* if you want to win.

Q. *How do you handle the problem of parents who interfere with your coaching?*

A. Every coach gets that. Everybody wants to be the coach—parents, brothers, sisters, girl friends. They all mean well. They're just trying to help the player, and you could make the point that if they succeed in improving the player, they are thus improving the team, but that's not necessarily so. I had a guy once, a real star, who was averaging twenty-seven points a game for us. Well his dad told his son that he should shoot more and then he'd average forty a game. That was fine, except it disrupted our whole offense, so I went to the father and we had a very candid discussion, one on one. When I explained the complications his advice was causing, he apologized. He then realized what I had meant when I had told him, "Your advice is almost ruining our team." The boy went back to team play, continued to score well and we were back on the track. Teamwork and team discipline: It's an emphasis I preach all the time, as do other coaches. Teamwork wins.

Q. *How do you feel about the slowdown, the Four Corners offense? Should this be allowed in high school and college ball, or should there be a twenty-four-second or thirty-second shot clock, like the twenty-four-second clock in the NBA?*

A. I would be for a thirty-second shot clock in high school and college, as long as the equipment wouldn't cost the school too much money to buy and install. I'd also eliminate the jump ball and merely take turns in what are now jump-ball situations. The visitors would get the ball out of bounds at the start of the game, then you'd alternate the rest of the game anytime the ball was tied up. There is room for improvement in the NBA, too. Those players are the greatest athletes in the world, in my opinion. They're not just a group of big men; they could succeed in other sports as well. The NBA has to clean up its act, however. It should eliminate the hand-checking and not just say it's being eliminated. It should cut out all the violence, the pushing and shoving and elbowing. That's not basketball and it doesn't take any skill to give somebody a chop from behind. The NBA could also restore half-court zone pressing and trapping. These strategies would add a new dimension to the pro game and bring a lot of variety to it that isn't there now. People say that if you've seen one regular season game in the NBA, you've seen them all.

Q. *The NBA has a "hardship" rule under which a college player can turn pro a year or two before his class graduates, or never even go to college, on the grounds that his family is suffering financial hardship and needs the money he'll make in pro ball. Do you think that's a good rule?*

A. Even though I encourage athletes to complete college, and emphasize it more than a lot of other coaches, I also feel a college athlete should be able to turn pro if he wants to—whenever he wants to—even if he might be making a mistake. In other words, he should have the right to make that mistake. He should also bear in mind, however, that he's taking two risks: one, that he may never return to get his degree, and he'll need that a lot more than he'll need anything else after he plays pro ball. He may last only a year or two in the pros; it's happened many times.

That's when that degree is the greatest insurance policy in the world. And two, that he won't get hurt. That's also happened to guys after they went hardship. I would discourage anyone from doing it, but it's their right if that's what they want.

Q. *What about All-Star games for high school players? Are they a good idea?*

A. I think they are a good idea, yes, but there are good All-Star games and bad ones. By that I mean no high school All-Star game should be played to make money for the promoters. They should be played to give the kids some healthy exposure to college scouts and to raise money for reputable charities. They shouldn't be flesh markets from which some hustler makes big money off teenagers playing a ball game.

The McDonald's All-American games are the best example I know of a high school All-Star game which is played the way they should be. The restaurant chain picks the best players in America—the McDonald's High School All-American Team—then plays a national game, East versus West, the twenty players divided into two squads of ten each. Proceeds go to a local charity in the city where the game is played. McDonald's also takes ten players from that squad and brings them to Washington to play our local All-Stars in the annual Capital Classic, with proceeds going to the Children's Hospital. They don't make one dime off those games. On the contrary, they have donated $150,000 to charity.

Another danger to look out for in All-Star games is kids playing in too many of them and missing too much high school time as a result. I don't think anyone should play in more than two. The coaches of these games can control that limit simply by refusing to allow a man to be put on his team if he's already accepted two or more invitations to play in other All-Star games. I've been suggesting to my coaching colleagues that all of us should be strict about this and everyone seems to agree. I think we'll be able to keep things from getting out of hand—by making sure we don't forget our priorities.

Q. *There is strong sentiment in some quarters for making the use of marijuana legal in the United States. Young people are especially vocal about it. How do you feel about this?*

A. I am flatly opposed to it. I don't think we should do it any more than we should put beer in school drinking fountains. Some kids—I repeat, *some* kids—might think that would be great, but that doesn't make it a good idea. Some kids would like to be able to get a driver's license at fourteen instead of sixteen, but that doesn't make that a good idea, either. I am opposed to the use of liquor or drugs by any student, and I'm opposed to the use of drugs, including marijuana, by anyone of any age. We don't know yet what its prolonged use can do to damage your body. That's one good reason right there. And there's no way it can be good for you. No way.

That's the same mentality which won a change in the laws of our state lowering the beer-drinking age from twenty-one to eighteen. That was another serious mistake. Drinking and drugs are not a serious problem at De-Matha, not to my knowledge, but any laws which are liberalized like that, if you can call it "liberalizing," are a threat to the health and well-being of all of us individually and of our society in general. I think I know a little bit about history, and I think I'm right when I say that making the use of marijuana legal is the kind of moral decay and cop-out that is both sinful and a threat to our continued greatness as a nation. Using marijuana never made anybody anything good.

Q. *You're a teacher, a coach and a father. What is the one specific piece of advice you might give parents?*

A. The most important thing you can give your children is your time. Spend your evenings with them, your weekends, your vacations. They're going to be gone soon enough anyhow, so enjoy them while you can, which at the same time tells them that you really care for them. Help them to be able to recognize the difference between good and evil and to realize that there *are* evil things in this life. There are good movies and there are movies which are just plain trash. There is good music and bad music, good TV shows and bad ones. Maybe it's helpful that there is evil in this life, because being able to recognize it and deal with it helps us to recognize the good things and to cherish and develop them. But you have to teach the difference, by spending time with them. I don't believe in the bumper-sticker approach to solving our problems, but there's one particular bumper sticker which offers a lot of food for thought for all of us, the one that says:

"Have you hugged your kid today?"

The record shows that DeMatha's coach practices what he preaches. He is willing not only to apply discipline whenever and wherever it is needed, but to place the importance of the lesson learned above the need to win another game if the issue is that critical. An example is the time he demoted his ninth-grade starter, Adrian Dantley, to the jayvee for "lack of maturity" after Dantley took advantage of Wootten's absence from practice one day to try to get away with a few things at the expense of Wootten's assistant. A few weeks later Dantley was called back up to the varsity, but he has said since that it was one of the best lessons anyone ever taught him.

Another example is the time Morgan found out three of his players had broken training by drinking beer after defeating the American University freshman team. He called a team meeting in one of the DeMatha classrooms, told the team what had happened and asked his players what they thought the penalty should be. The violators were named, and an open discussion followed, during which All-American Brendan McCarthy spoke up: "Coach, I just want to say that whatever penalty is imposed on these guys should also be imposed on me, because they came by my house and I would have gone with them, but my mother wouldn't let me." Everybody laughed, but the penalty was handed down anyhow: The players could stay on the team, but they were sentenced to a considerable amount of extra running in the form of sprints and baseline-to-baseline "double suicides."

Rocco Mennella, the chairman of DeMatha's mathematics department, remembers a game, too, against Gaithersburg High School in neighboring Montgomery County, Maryland, when Wootten put the need to learn a lesson above the need to win. Hawkeye Whitney, then a ninth grader, was in the stands, suspended from the team for disciplinary reasons.

DeMatha was in trouble late in the game when Morgan turned around to his young star and said, "We sure could use a big man in there." But Mennella remembers that Wootten never called Whitney down to the bench to tell him to get dressed and rush in there and save the game. "DeMatha lost," Mennella says today, "but a lesson was learned. Hawkeye was a model student and player for the rest of his four years here. Morgan was showing us that no victory is so valuable that a coach should forfeit his opportunity and his responsibility to teach a lesson to a boy who needs it."

———————————

"... to Touch People's Lives"

You've got to accentuate the positive,
Eliminate the negative,
Latch on to the affirmative,
Don't mess with Mister Inbetween.*

Like Bear Bryant and Alabama, Tom Landry and the Dallas Cowboys, the Morgan Wootten–DeMatha marriage is so ideal it is hard to imagine either of them apart from the other. It has endured for twenty-three years despite the efforts of many colleges to lure him away to a big-time job. The list includes at least three schools in the Atlantic Coast Conference and one NCAA champion.

The closest call of all came in March, 1969, when the University of Maryland was seriously recruiting both Morgan and Lefty Driesell of Davidson College in North Carolina for its vacancy as head basketball coach. Things finally got to the point where Morgan said he would take the job if Lefty, Maryland's first choice, turned it down. The weekend that Driesell was to announce his decision happened to be the weekend of one of DeMatha's greatest basketball triumphs: That Saturday, James Brown had collapsed on the bench during the Knights of Columbus tournament at Maryland and had been taken to the hospital. The next day, with Brown gone, McKinley Tech was supposed to mop up DeMatha for the title. As Wootten has described, some of his friends actually called to beg off going to the game, saying they couldn't stand the thought of seeing De-Matha not only defeated but embarrassed. As it happened, Mark Edwards, only six four, spent the afternoon outrebounding two Tech players each four inches taller than he was and DeMatha won in a romp.

In the fourth quarter, with DeMatha ahead by twenty-two points, the game was decided, but the Maryland coaching question was not. DeMatha's coach, awed by the effort his players were making in behalf of their fallen teammate, put his head on his hands on the De-Matha bench and prayed silently, "Please, God, let Lefty take the job."

At Ledo's Restaurant later that afternoon, his more loyal friends still with him, Morgan was celebrating with a victory dinner when he was interrupted by a telephone call. It was Mark Asher of the *Washington Post*. "Morgan," he said, "Lefty's taking the Maryland job. He just announced it on his TV show at Davidson."

His prayer had been answered. The next day, Lefty Driesell was at DeMatha, trying to recruit James Brown for Maryland.

Mark Edwards, one of the heroes of that still-remembered upset over Tech, remembers something else about that time at DeMatha. He calls it "the openness of De-Matha's athletes and student body," more particularly what people call racial harmony. Mark Edwards is a graduate of Georgetown University now, an actor and producer. He's also black. In some schools in the 1960s, in those days of riots in Watts and Cambridge and Detroit, the assassination of Martin Luther King and "long, hot summers," racial harmony was noticeably absent, but at DeMatha everyone lived together and worked together. It had to do with what so many people call "the DeMatha Family."

Mark's coach remembers one time in particular when DeMatha was returning to Hyattsville after an afternoon game in nearby Baltimore. The team stopped at a restaurant on Route 29 for dinner. The owner, spotting the black players among the whites, pulled Morgan Wootten aside and told him the blacks would have to eat in another room. Before their coach could answer, his players—all of them, black and white—stood up at the same time and left, without saying a word, a unanimous reflex action.

That superb effort against the odds in defeating McKinley Tech, and that team action in the restaurant, are but two examples of the way Wootten's players react to his guidance of them both as athletes and as men. One of the favorite poems that Wootten distributes every year to his players and to the kids in his summer camp is Rudyard Kipling's "If." Several stanzas seem to describe what the Wootten-DeMatha program strives to instill:

If you can keep your head when all about you
Are losing theirs, and blaming it on you,

If you can trust yourself when all men doubt you,
But make allowance for their doubting too; . . .

If you can dream—and not make dreams your master;
If you can think—and not make thoughts your aim;

If you can meet with triumph and disaster
And treat those two imposters just the same; . . .

Or watch the things you gave your life to broken,
And stoop and build 'em up with worn-out tools; . . .

If you can force your heart and nerve and sinew
To serve your turn long after they are gone,

And so hold on when there is nothing in you
Except the Will which says to them: "Hold on";

If you can talk with crowds and keep your virtue
Or walk with Kings—nor lose the common touch; . . .

If you can fill the unforgiving minute
With sixty seconds' worth of distance run—

Yours is the Earth and everything that's in it,
And—which is more—you'll be a Man, my son.

There is another poem as well which must be quoted here, a poem which sums up the essence of what Wootten believes in. It comes from no famous writer, but from a resident of Urbana, Illinois, over one hundred years old, who sent it to John Wooden. Wooden in turn sent it to Morgan. It's called "What Is Success?" and these are its last three stanzas:

You must learn that it's true and really believe
That it's more blessed to give than it is to receive.
Then, giving all that you have, in whatever you do,
In service for others, will bring success to you.

It is not what you do or get while you live
But what you become and the service you give.
Your doing and getting are but the process of living,
Your success is achieved in becoming and giving.

What kind of a person are you becoming each day?
What kind of a world will result from your way?
Answer these questions. Put yourself to the test.
By their answers alone can we measure success.

Wootten makes no apologies for his love of such works and his distribution of them. Instead, he insists they are an essential ingredient in developing those "good people" he is convinced are the first requirement of any successful program.

If some people want to call that corny, Morgan Wootten is the last person to let it bother him. Instead, he lets his record speak for itself: all those wins, all of those championships and, most of all in his order of priorities, all of those college graduates produced through his program.

For, far more than well-rounded athletes, what Morgan Wootten wants to produce is well-rounded human beings. Ask him what his greatest reward from coaching is and he answers, "The opportunity to teach—to touch people's lives." DeMatha Principal John Moylan once told Dave Krider of *Basketball Weekly*, "People don't believe this, but he's a better teacher than coach. The one reason he's so successful is he's a very fine teacher— the very best." He works hard at it, finds genuine satisfaction in it and is especially gratified when he learns that he influenced a person's life in a helpful way without even knowing it.

Folded away in the back of a book in the Wootten household is a letter received in 1976 from a John M. Fantone, operations officer of the First National Bank of Tampa, Florida. Mr. Fantone never knew Morgan well, never played for him, never even went to DeMatha. Morgan in turn can barely remember what he did for the man. Still, there in the letter is this tribute:

> I was a player for another school and I will always be grateful to you for seeing to my needs in my senior year at Saint Anthony's. If it hadn't been for your efforts, I would not have been able to attend college and possibly would not hold the position that I do now. I often wonder how much more successful I would have been if I had attended DeMatha High School.

And then there is this letter, from a boy named Michael O'Brien at Coffeyville Junior College in Kansas, received in 1964. It seems a fitting note on which to close this book.

Dear Morgan,

I want to express my deep thanks to you for showing the confidence in me to provide an opportunity for a college education. Your call to Tulsa University on my behalf opened the door for me here at Coffeyville.

I'll be the first in my family to receive a degree. My parents came from Ireland and have always hoped that their children would go to the university. I called my mother yesterday and she is receiving radiation treatments for her cancer. When I told her I wanted to come home and be with her, she told me, "Don't let Coach Wootten down. Stay out there and do your best."

Well, Morgan, I know if I do well on the team and in the classroom you will be able to call Coach Ball and recommend another city kid for a scholarship and a chance for an education.

Thanks again for extending your hand in friendship to someone who wasn't even on your team but someone who you believed would be a credit to you and the program at DeMatha.

Sincerely,
Michael O'Brien

That's the Morgan Wootten story—in only four paragraphs.